LESSONS LIVED OUT

A 1-Year Weekly Devotional

Presented by R. S. Dugan

For information contact :
SPIRIT & TRUTH
PO BOX 1737
MARTINSVILLE, IN 46151
spiritandtruthonline.org

Book and Cover design by Rodjie Ulanday
ISBN: 978-0-578-31401-3

First Edition: December 2021

10 9 8 7 6 5 4 3 2 1

INTRODUCTION

by R. S. Dugan

Back in late 2016-early 2017, I found myself in something of a spiritual wilderness. I was stagnating in my walk, not really sure where I fit in amongst my peers and coworkers. By that time, I had been serving in ministry work for almost a decade, but had yet to figure out what that looked like for me in the longterm. I wasn't much of a teacher, my brain didn't hold Bible facts very well, and the few times I'd written articles as a teen, the constructive critique I received left me heartbroken and afraid to try again (I hadn't yet developed the thick skin necessary for professional writing). I thought I was good at only one thing—novel writing—and did not ever see my two worlds of secular fiction and spiritual work colliding.

Then, in the midst of my wilderness, a hand reached out. One of my mentors, Dan Gallagher, invited me to contribute any time I wanted to Spirit & Truth's blog—at the time, primarily populated by him. I was an avid reader and the primary editor of the blog at the time, but didn't consider myself "spiritual" enough to put my voice out there. What did an early-20's girl have to say to the world?

Fortunately, as is usually the case, God had a plan I could've never foreseen. All He needed was someone to give me that boost.

I wrote my first blog in response to a devastating wildfire that personally affected someone my family knew. Then I got another idea thanks to a video game I was playing at the time. Then something leaped out of my battle with anxiety and that wilderness wandering of my soul. And then it sort of snowballed, as things often do when they have God's hand on them.

Within a few years, I'd become a regular contributor the blog; and then, by 2020, I myself was its primary writer. Through a series of mentors and encouragers in my life, I finally found my voice—the same voice God gave me to tell stories was the voice He intended to minister through these short-but-sweet, heartfelt pieces.

Not too long after I first hit my stride with these blogs, around 2018, God gave me the heads-up that this was just the beginning; He gave me a vision to compile these writings into a devotional to touch even more hearts and lives. I fostered that vision for years and years, waiting until the right time.

What you hold in your hands now is the realization of that vision...that the time has finally come. In mid-2021, five years after I began writing for the Spirit & Truth blog and just after I returned from maternity leave, God placed the pressure on my heart: it was time to revisit and update this devotional, and then offer it to the world.

So, what can you expect to find between these pages? Perhaps not your typical devotional content! "Lessons Lived Out" is anecdotal as well as instructional. It forays down the path of a lifelong Christian still figuring out her place in the Body of Christ. It's something of a breadcrumb path—a look into the outcome of my wilderness journey with God as my guide. Here you'll find insights from a writer who spent many long and difficult months figuring out how to use her voice for Christ, and in each week's installment you'll find the musings, humor, questions, life experiences, and ultimately the lessons God taught me along the way.

I pray these lessons lived out will encourage, inspire, and uplift you, that they'll make you smile, laugh, maybe even cry (in a good way); and also that they'll prompt you to think, to reflect, and to look ahead with renewed vision.

I pray you find exactly what you need here, however alike or dissimilar our experiences may be. I pray the voice that God gave me speaks to you; and I pray that yours is one of the hearts and lives He knew would be touched by this devotional.

God bless you!
R. S. Dugan

PASSING THROUGH THE FIRE

When you walk through the fire, you will not be scorched,
Nor will the flame burn you...
(Isaiah 43:2)

IN THE LATE FALL OF 2016, arsonists set a wildfire ablaze in the Smokey Mountains near Pigeon Forge and Gatlinburg, Tennesee. It burned hundreds of acres, took several lives, destroyed many homes and businesses, and threatened countless more. All told, it cost the region hundreds of thousands of dollars and placed a severe strain on a beautiful swath of the midsouth that relies heavily on tourist traffic to thrive. At the advent of Christmas, a time of celebration and cheer, many were picking apart rubble rather than presents, trying to piece together a new life instead of a new gadget, and sifting through the ashes like newly-fallen snow.

Even those not living in the region were affected. Not long after the fires began to burn, family friends informed us that they had lost vacation homes to the blaze—real estate they'd poured blood, sweat, tears, and money into in the interest of reaping income back from renting them out. Months of loving labor, gone up in smoke.

Not all of us will face the horrors of arson or accidental fires, but in the grand scheme of things, we all get burned. Loss, tragedy, sickness, death, hardships, and suffering are all infernos we're forced to confront in some way or another, and they never leave us unscathed.

When you're standing blistered and scorched on the other side of the heat, it's difficult to see the fire as anything other than a merciless thief. But not every inferno is meant to burn us alive. Flames can cleanse as well as kill, and heat purifies. There is a refiner's fire that comes from the hand of God—one that will test the very foundations our lives are built on, and the durability of the works we have done, for good or for bad.

Someday, we all face fire; and when we pass through it on the Day of Judgement, we'll be left standing on the other side as soil enriched by the nitrous of the flames, all the darkness stripped from our bones. What grows back will be greater than what was before; the pain of the fire will fade as God, in His mercy, helps us flourish again.

The next time you're faced with the fires of this world, with the heat against your face and underneath your skin, remember that you will emerge on the other side. You will face the aftermath. And in spite of everything, you *can* regrow—with the help of a powerful and mighty God, perhaps even better than before.

This Week's Prayer: God, please lead me through the fires of this life and help me emerge stronger than ever! Help me remember You can bring good from the hardest times. Refine me and make me even greater at following and serving You. Amen.

SAFE IN THE MASTER'S ARMS

The name of the Lord is a strong tower; the righteous runs
into it and is safe.
(Proverbs 18:10)

MY BROTHER ONCE UNDERTOOK A brief stint
of dog-sitting for his roommate, Jerry, who was out
of town. I should preface this tale by saying that my
brother is, above all things, *not* a dog person. He is

especially not a dog person when it comes to dogs with separation anxiety, which this dog, Dexter, unfortunately struggled with. The two managed to come to an agreement after some finagling and restless nights, and despite long days parted from his Person, Dexter pulled through the anxious week until he was reunited with his master.

Several days after Jerry's return, we all got together to watch a movie with pizza and popcorn—a classic Saturday night. And, content with having been the center of attention (at least mine!) for most of the day, Dexter settled happily in Jerry's lap, stretched out, and promptly fell into a deep, snoring sleep. At a break in the movie's action, my brother looked over and laughed, "That's the most relaxed I've seen that dog in a week."

"How so?" I asked.

"He just looks so—I dunno. Like he feels completely safe."

As I watched Dexter blissfully snore away, I realized it was true. And it wasn't the first time he'd displayed so much complete trust and devotion to his Person, either. Dexter and Jerry wrestled and chased each other constantly; Jerry could scoop Dexter up off the floor, flop him on his back, hang him upside down, rub his belly, hug him and get hugged back—even toss him up and catch him like a toddler! And Dexter never showed an ounce of fear, only tail-wagging joy. He was content, feeling safe no matter what happened to him as long as he was in his master's trustworthy hands.

A dog that's loved and cherished and *knows* it, like Dexter, sets a pretty great example of how our relationship with God should be. When we truly *understand*, when we unequivocally *believe* in God's love for us—that He catches us when we fall, that He does what He does out of care and commitment to us, that He adores and provides for us, and that He will absolutely never, *ever* harm us, under any circumstances—we experience a peace that surpasses understanding.

And when that happens, then we can find rest after troubling times...safely back in the Master's arms.

This Week's Prayer: God, please help me to remember I am safest in Your arms. When I'm tempted to stray, lead me back. Shelter and guide me always. Amen.

HERE COMES THE SUN

Now we know that in all things God works for the good of
those who love him...
(Romans 8:28)

IN THE EARLY WINTER OF 2017, the state of
Indiana experienced one of the longest stretches of
overcast weather in recent memory. For weeks on
end, nothing but dreary clouds crowded the sky. Any
hint of sunlight above came between thick banks of
clouds like a sly wink, an "Ah-ha, gotcha!" before the

murkiness resumed. It became a coping mechanism for my family to joke about the sun like it was some long-lost artifact of a bygone, happier age.

"What's the sun? Isn't it that huge, glowing ball that legend tells once lived in the sky? Yes, I seem to recall the stories about it...tales from long, long ago..."

Despite our jabs at humor, we never actually doubted that the sun was up there. The proof of its existence remained in the fact that it went from "pitch black" to "tolerably murky" every morning. Even if 7 a.m. still looked like midnight, and the 8 a.m. sunrise like the 5 p.m. sunset, we knew the sun was out there, planning to peak.

Cloudy days come and go; sometimes when the sun is high in the sky, it's still hidden behind the shadows of our personal struggles. The deep darkness of life can come upon us without warning. In those times, it's often difficult to see the sun for the clouds...to remember that even in those times of hardship, God is still present. But just as we never doubt that the sun is rising and falling behind the slip of the shade, we're charged in our faith to never doubt that God, too, is working behind the veil, warming and growing the world, taking an active role in our lives even when we don't see His hand at play.

It's out there. It's still happening.

When the cloudy days come—and they always do— nothing is more challenging than the fight to keep our eyes and minds fixed on the hope and promise of a

Father who hasn't abandoned us. But no matter how cloudy the skies, we should always work hard to guard and maintain our trust. Even when things seem hopeless, without a hint of sunlight in sight, we have a promise of a God who will never leave us or forsake us; so we know that the clouds will eventually pass on. And if we continue to strive forward through life's shadows, keeping our gazes fixed ahead, we will catch a wink from above...the reassuring smile of our Heavenly Father at work behind the scenes, reminding us in His perfect way that we will reach the light. He is with us, no matter the darkness.

The clouds will pass. And then we see the sun.

This Week's Prayer: God, please help me remember the storms of life don't last forever! Help me see beyond the clouds to the light of Your glory. Give me a heavenly perspective even on the darkest days. Amen.

BATTERD SHIPS SAIL ON

*Count it all joy when you encounter trials of various kinds,
knowing that the testing of your trust produces endurance.*
(James 1:2-3)

IN MY EARLY TWENTIES, I hit a stagnant place in my spiritual walk. It happens, like with just about anything else—even in the things in life we love most. We plateau; we lose focus, get distracted by other things. But what made these spiritual doldrums

4

different for me was that this time it was more of a "conscious separation" than a careless wandering.

It came on the heels of a particularly rough beginning to the year, where my manageable anxiety exploded into full-on, crippling panic episodes that left me feeling like I was going to die. Amidst a storm of emotions that to this day I still can't completely articulate, the most prominent was a reccurring certainty that my walk with God was going to end in the death and devastation of everything I cared about. Like a modern-day Job, my walk with Christ was going to cost it all—my family's lives, my friendships, my pets, even the breath in my lungs.

So my battered brain's solution was to take the easy way out. I figured if I backed off on the spiritual battle I'd been fighting so hard to wage, I'd somehow prolong everyone's lives and prevent bad things from happening. Take the target off myself and my family, so to speak. I know this position isn't unique to me— I've heard it espoused by many before, and I was defeated enough to try it. Feeling completely worn-down from a rough year fighting my own head, I figured I deserved a break.

But after several months where I straddled the line between responsible and rote, doing the bare minimum to eke by on faith while still trying to distance myself from a battle I no longer felt equipped to fight, God brought to my attention the fact that I wasn't actually reducing the target on myself by shrinking back. We don't protect ourselves by living lukewarm faith, trying to shuffle along through the shadows unnoticed by the Enemy. We're called to fight, not to cower; and like ships on a sea rolling in the battle between good and evil, we're part of a much larger fleet. We're called to hold our ground, defend our vessel, and protect the ships around us. Our lives, sanctified, sworn to Christ, serve such an unbelievably high purpose, and we are a threat to the Enemy. To withhold ourselves out of fear is a disservice to the flag we fight beneath.

To live is Christ. To die, even to die fighting, is gain. And no matter what chaos and strife the battle brings our way, it's a far better Life ahead than what lies behind. So we must sail on.

This Week's Prayer: God, please strengthen and sustain me through life's battles! Give me the courage to endure even in the hardest times. Help me to remember that I'm not alone in this fight and that yours is a cause worth fighting for. Amen.

UNPLUGGED!

Peace I leave with you; my peace I give you. I do not give to
you as the world gives.
(John 14:27)

OPINIONS ARE LIKE BUTTS: everyone's got one.

Since the dawn of creation, mankind has always had an opinion about *something*. As much as God might've wished He hadn't included that in our makeup after listening to the Israelites complaining about their opinions of life in the wilderness for forty years, He still loved us enough to give us free will that allows us to form opinions.

And boy, do we. About *everything*.

In the not-too-distant past, the platforms from which a man could flaunt his opinion were generally relegated to whatever social circle he moved in. Families, close friends, and maybe a few gossips around town got the scoop on what Joe Cool was thinking about anything under the sun. Politicians, stars, and socialites had a broader circle, but those of opined minds in different spheres still didn't rub shoulders as much.

Then came the internet.

Sharing one's opinion has become an Olympic sport for which many, *many* people seem to be training toward the gold. From politicians to celebrities to the next sensationalist post just down the superhighway, everyone's personal insight into everything is always just one clickbait away. That's not even to mention the opinions of those we consider friends or acquaintances. As the saying goes, you can't swing a dead skunk in a social-media circle without hitting someone who has a different opinion (or something like that).

With the addition of keyboard courage, which makes even the humblest fingers light up with the fires of righteously raging internet justice, it's pretty much impossible to even boot up your computer without having someone else's opinion lobbed in your face.

Once technology becomes self-aware, I'm sure it'll be sharing its opinions on startup, too.

Flashback to late 2016: with the United States elections upcoming, the political landscape became a bloodbath. I witnessed several Facebook friends being swept up in argument after argument, resulting in politically-induced anxiety that bled over into their day-to-day lives. Everyone's opinion about what everyone *else* should think, believe, feel, and follow was plastered on their walls and each other's newsfeeds. Fed up with the whole circus, my husband deleted his Facebook. His stress levels were immediately much lower, and I could see why. We claim that everything these days is lobbying to steal our peace, but how much of that stress do we actually willfully bring on ourselves by what we allow into our lives?

I encourage you to take a step back, evaluate, and ask, "How much of this stress am I heaping on *myself*? How much could I avoid if I just unplugged, even for one or two days a week? If I spent that time doing something that relaxes me, would I honestly be any worse off? Do I *need* the arguments and high blood pressure?"

I know when I've asked myself this, the answer has always been a big, resounding *NOPE*. I wouldn't be worse off—in fact, the times when I've unplugged for twenty-four hours, I've discovered something wonderful: the world keeps spinning. My day-to-day life doesn't change when I'm oblivious to friends X, Y, and Z's rants for the day. That's not to say we all need to delete our Facebooks, our Twitters, and our email addresses, but healthy balance is good for the body from the inside out.

Above all, when we unplug our chargers from the chaos of the world, we're so much freer to plug into God—the only source of power that *truly* recharges us and gives us strength to face tomorrow.

This Week's Prayer: God, please help me discern the things in life I need to "unplug" from! Give me the strength and willpower to let go of what stresses my body and clutters my mind. Help me to plug into You so I can be recharged to do Your will. Amen.

THE IMPORTANCE OF CHOICE

"See, I have set before you today life and good, death and evil.
(Deuteronomy 30:15)

THE POWER TO CHOOSE IS considered by most to be an inherent human right, albeit addressed from differing positions depending on religious, political, and social customs. But sometimes it feels like with all the freedom we possess—especially those of us who have a multitude of choices for everything from our breakfast cereal to our college options to our tombstone materials—we forget just how important the sheer *freedom of choice* actually is.

God places so much emphasis on the beauty of choice, both in His actions toward us and in His Word. Think about how many people both harmed and helped the cause of God's people by the choices they made: kings and counsellors who walked with God or fell away all shaped history as we know it; pious individuals and pagans made decisions that changed the face of life for those in their time as well as their descendants for generations after.

God could've just as easily designed a universe where we were all slaves, bound by the laws of the universe to serve Him. Instead He chose to give us *free will*, the chance to *choose* to love Him. Jesus' sacrifice on the Cross is made all the more powerful by the fact that he *chose* to endure that suffering. Even while he was hanging by the nails in his hands, he could've called a battalion of angels to rescue him, yet he chose to see it through to the end. In addition:

- Eve and Adam chose to eat the fruit.
- Rahab chose to hide the spies.
- Moses chose to go back to Egypt.
- Peter chose to deny Christ.

Rather than puppets pulled on strings held by a bored Creator, we are individuals free to think and act however we see fit—sometimes for good, sometimes for bad. But thank God we *have* the choice to love Him, to seek Him, to hold fast to Him. We can choose to accept Christ as the sacrifice for our sins...or we can choose to carry the weight of sin for ourselves when we stand before the Creator.

How much more praise would we give our Creator if we truly understood the depth of love that exists in Him, an Author who allows things to play to the outcome of our choices, good and bad, that influence the Greatest Story.

This Week's Prayer: God, thank You so much for giving us free will! Help me to use that freedom in ways that glorify and honor You and Your Son and that help take care of Your people. Please lead me to wise choices and straight paths. Amen.

REPLAY

I have hidden your speech in my heart, so that I might not sin against you.
(Psalm 119:11)

RAISE YOUR HAND IF YOU have ever gotten a song stuck in your head.

We can all put our hands down now. Every single person has likely gotten a tune stuck in their head at some point. This isn't always a bad thing, especially if it's a song you love. But try listening to a record loop of The Hokey Pokey sung by your own brain for six hours; you'll be ready to put up a For Rent sign and vacate your head just to escape it.

Do you think Jesus ever got a song stuck in his head? Picture the scene: on the road between cities with not a lot but wilderness around them, and the disciples too weary to take another parable. Suddenly Jesus starts humming, and Peter's groaning, "Rabbi, *please...*!" and everyone has *A Lament of the Sons of Korah* stuck in their heads until they roll into Galilee.

Okay, maybe not. But the Bible gives us a look into what *was* actually looping in Jesus' brain throughout his ministry: *Scripture*. This earworm of godly facts allowed him to do some pretty powerful things like resist the Devil's temptations in the desert, liberate the oppressed masses with the truth of the Law and God's heart for mankind, and even elucidate his own place in prophecy and history up to the moment he was hanging on the cross!

Jesus didn't memorize Scripture because it was a necessity to be the perfect Man; it seems more likely that it was out of dedication to his Father and his calling in life that he devoted so much headspace to the Torah, the tales of his ancestors, and the writings of the prophets.

Imagine Jesus, up late into the night, reading and researching long after everyone else had gone to sleep.

He approached the Word of God with a passion that was personal—a hunger not foisted on him by a religious edict that told him he *had* to read a certain number of lines for a certain amount of time each day, but born from the deep well of his own excitement and relationship with God.

There's never any shortage of people who tell us how, when, and why to read the Bible. But to make it personal, it has to be a connective thread between us and God. Learning to truly enjoy the Bible as we seek the heart and will of the Father is a powerful, life-changing, and moving experience. So is scripture memorization, commiting certain passages to memory that have a powerful impact on our hearts and minds.

When we take the time to delve into the Bible, to spend enough time in it that it really becomes *real* to us—not just words on a page, but *life-giving Word* from our Heavenly Father—we are strengthened. Our spiritual walk is enhanced, and we're better equipped for the battle against evil with the full armor of God at our disposal.

Not only that, but when we take the time to commit Scripture to memory, we're prepared to deflect the fiery darts of the Enemy—the arrows of worthlessness, deception, falsehood, misdirection, misguidance and heresy.

And when we memorize scripture, we can catch the same earworm Jesus had—the one that sets our Father's truths on constant replay.

This Week's Prayer: God, thank You for Your wonderful Word! Please expand and strengthen my mind to retain more and more scripture, so I'm never without Your Word hidden within me. Amen.

TO WALK BESIDE A FRIEND

**A person has many friends to socialize with, but there is one
who loves him who stays closer than a brother.
(Proverbs 18:24)**

FOR MANY YEARS, I TOOK a 20-minute walk
through the neighborhood behind my house before
heading to the office. This gave me time to burn off
the energy of my morning coffee while I
brainstormed whatever novel I was currently writing,

and it put me at the doors right at the start of the workday. But on bitterly cold mornings when the wind blew strong, sometimes I cheated and walked straight to work instead because, let's face it, it's too cold to justify all that nonsense.

On one particular morning that was just slightly on the abominably cold side, I skipped my routine walk and just happened to meet a dog who was walking across the parking lot of a business half a block from work. I called him over and he came running for an ear-scratching, then tagged along at my heels as I walked. No matter how far he strayed to sniff dirt mounds or check the messages at our property's lonely fire hydrant, he always came jogging back to fall into step right beside me, all the way to the office door. This gave me a sense of security that was sometimes absent as I walked through the industrial park alone.

The experience got me reflecting on just how important it is to be part of a group. Even just two people (or a girl and a dog!) walking together can feel safer than being alone. It provides a sense of camaraderie, protection, and "safety in numbers". It gives us someone to talk to and share our time with (even if, as in my case, you're talking to a canine).

During his time of ministry, Jesus very rarely traveled alone, and the records of the Gospels paint a picture of a Rabbi who abounded with proverbs and parables that he often told to his followers *as they walked*.

In Jesus' darkest hour of greatest need, he even brought his disciples with him to the Garden of Gethsemane, where he then went off a ways to pray. And once his friends had scattered, he still wasn't alone; his Father was with him.

Sometimes I think we forget we're not alone, either.

Just like the men on the road to Emmaus, Jesus walks beside *us*, too. He's as close as a prayer, as a quiet conversation on a calm, chilly morning. Often when it feels like God and Christ are far away, it's because *we've* put distance there; but even when that happens, closing the breach is as simple as telling them, "I need you here."

No matter how far we've strayed, we can curve right back and walk side by side with them. God's love is redemptive. It's a correctional love, but also a protective one. He has defended His people countless times throughout the ages, walking beside them, preparing them, helping them face their problems.

Whatever need, whatever obstacle, whatever sense of loneliness and distance overtakes our hearts, we must always remember that "not even death or life, angels or rulers, things present or things to come, hostile powers, height or depth, or any other created thing will have the power to separate us from the love of God that is in Christ Jesus our Lord!"

This Week's Prayer: God, thank You for never forsaking me! Thank You for your constant presence in my life and for the holy spirit you sent to help comfort and guide us. Help me to be aware of Your presence in new and powerful ways.

Amen.

RULES OF THE ROAD

"If you love me, you will keep my commandments..."
(John 14:15)

GROWING UP IN INDIANA, THERE have been countless times where some outing or activity has required me to travel on "The Loop" – the local name for I-465, a massive 3-to-6-lane highway that encompasses the downtown Indianapolis area. By some madness (or because of on-ramps I suppose), the speed limit on this superhighway is 55 MPH, but no one ever, *ever* abides by that.

In fact, I'm pretty sure you'd have to be going against traffic, sacrificing a goat, or wielding a machete—possibly all three at the same time—to get pulled over on 465. The cops frequenting that highway just don't seem bothered at all that everyone does between 65-70 MPH at any given time.

While sailing down The Loop one day on the way back from visiting a friend, I watched a cop breeze past me doing at least 80, while other drivers around *him* were going close to 85, and I was struck by the realization that there are some rules we just naturally don't obey. Even with a hard-and-fast speed limit, on any given road there's the unspoken rule that going "five over" isn't punishable. Technically, it's breaking the law, but there's an understanding in place. In fact, in Indiana, there's a *new* law that if you're *not doing five over in the fast lane*, you can get pulled over!

We play loose with a lot of rules, especially in modern society. Not picking up after our dogs on walks, loitering, jaywalking—let's face it, we've all bent the law at some point. But even in our rush to get home, to keep walking the dog, to cross the street, etc., we do ourselves a disservice if we ever forget *why* those laws are in place. The number of times the local news has played stories of cars completely totaled in 70 MPH wrecks on The Loop while harried motorists were trying desperately to cross five lanes of traffic to reach their exit is just sobering.

The entire universe operates on a system of natural and supernatural laws. The Law of Gravity is one we really don't have a choice but to abide by. On the other hand, the *supernatural* laws—God's laws—aren't a ball-and-chain. We aren't forced into purity, clean speech, or holiness of thought. We can play loose with those laws if we choose to, but like a speed limit, they are in place for a *reason*.

Our actions have consequences, some of which are readily apparent. Others have fallout we can't fathom at the time, with effects that ripple out both in the physical and spiritual realms. That's when we really have to trust God and trust His laws...trust that they were put in place not to hinder us, but to keep us from wrecking out at 70 MPH and possibly taking innocent people down with us.

In the end, it never benefits us to break God's laws. These guidelines are there for our spiritual and physical safety; our loving Father put them in place to keep us clean, pure, and safe. And while the laws of man can be unjust, unwarranted, and even cruel, the laws of God are always righteous, necessary, and fair. They're there for our protection, and for the safety of others who can be harmed by our sin in ways we just don't foresee.

It's true that speeding toward something, cutting corners, and playing loose with the laws can get us where we're going faster—but only God's way is guaranteed to get us there in one piece!

This Week's Prayer: God, thank You for Your rules and boundaries that help me lead the most fruitful life possible. Please help me to always be mindful and respectful of them. And please show me where I begin to stray from Your safe way! Amen.

FIVE WAYS TO FACE FEAR

For God gave us a spirit not of fear but of power and love and self-control.
(2 Timothy 1:7)

IT'S A PART OF THE human condition that ultimately, we all fear *something*. From quiet unease to life-altering phobias, we've all faced it at some point. As a society, 2020 and the COVID-19 pandemic scenario brought unique opportunities for people to come face-to-face with how they deal with fear. There were those who found their capacity to handle fear was a lot higher than they realized; others were unable to live a normal life, with terror pressing in on all sides.

Everyone has reasons for reacting to fear the way they do. But one of the greatest problems with fear is that it greatly hinders our effectiveness on God's behalf. If you've experienced this, you likely have found yourself wanting to switch up your "fear response and emotional energy" – you want to be FREE from the crippling grip of fear!

Below are five key strategies to tackle fear in such a way that it honors both God Himself, and your personal walk with the Lord!

1. Understand that God Loves You!

One of the greatest challenges that Christians face— and that stops nonbelievers from coming to a place of salvation—is the fear that God is angry with them. So many broken hearts remain enslaved to shame, unable to be set free because of a deep suspicion that God hates them. Some of the boldest steps to escaping the bondage of fear can be taken once we truly grasp that God *loves* us despite our shortcomings. When we lay our trust in God, we're able to set aside the fear that He is resentful, angry, or disgusted with us, and the peace that comes from that knowledge will allow us to dig deeper and unpack the rest of our fears.

Additionally, when we work out our relationship with God from a foundation of love rather than doubt, it allows us to see how He is working for our good in every scenario! Consequently, that makes things a lot LESS scary!

2. Recognize What Fear Actually Is

Fear is a visceral and chemical reaction to a *perception of danger or discomfort*. While it's good to have a healthy respect for things such as snakes or spiders, or for a shady block of the street where you shouldn't walk at night, **fear itself** doesn't equip you to face these things. In fact, fear can inhibit your ability to rationally face the things that endanger you! In short, fear can't save you.

Thankfully, while we can't control the circumstances that bring *about* fear, we can control fear itself by controlling our minds. When we make it our default to entrust our worries to God rather than holding onto them, and instead think rationally about what we can and cannot do about a situation, fear begins to lose its grip. Trust and logic take precedence over the perception of danger as something we must face all on our own!

3. Embrace God's Truth About Fear

It's interesting that one of the first signs of sin nature having come to rest in the spirit of Adam was that he was **afraid because he was naked**, so he hid from God. Before the Fall of Man, Adam and Eve lived fearlessly among the lions and wolves. They spoke with God, unafraid. All of that changed when sin entered the world; between the pages of Scripture there began a campaign, carried out by God from Abram all the way to Mary, from Hagar all the way to Samuel, and to all of Israel, to the disciples of Jesus, and to all of us now: "**Do not be afraid**," God said. And later, through Christ, "**God has not given us a spirit of fearfulness.**" Fear hinders us from being effective witnesses and warriors for God; God knows this, and He's equipped us to face fear through power, love, and ultimately, sound-mindedness.

There is also a spiritual element to fear – a "spirit of fear" or a "spirit of timidity/intimidation". When frightened thoughts start to intrude, rebuke them in the name of Jesus! You have authority in him, and there is power in his name; don't hesitate to come against fear from that place of spiritual power in the name of Jesus and tear down those spiritual strongholds in your heart and mind!

4. Don't Be Impressed by Fear

This was a lesson I learned from an account by Dave Meyer, husband of renowned Christian speaker Joyce

Meyer. In it, Dave talks about his childhood and adolescent struggles with migraine headaches. He began to dread the first signs of the migraines—blurry vision—because he knew what followed. One day, at the onset of yet another migraine, he heard God clearly tell him, "Don't be impressed by it."

What a powerful lesson! When we give over to a sense of fear, what we're really doing is allowing the idea of danger or harm to *impress itself upon us*. Like a wet, suffocating blanket, it smothers our rationality and occludes our common sense. But when the first tangles of fear start to weave into our minds, we have the choice to say, "I won't fear this. I won't let it impress me. I'm going to face this logically and respectfully and look for a solution."

5. Face Fear Head-On

While facing the things that *make* us afraid isn't always simple, facing fear itself is actually a straightforward process. We have the choice to meet the front lines of our dread, or to flee. When we choose to flee, we don't conquer fear, it conquers *us*. We cower from it, and that means the next time it comes back, it will inevitably have "grown" in our minds. On the other hand, when we choose to face fear and remind ourselves that this is a *feeling*, a *thought* that can be led captive in obedience to Christ, to the love of God, and to the truths He tells us about fear, we have a victory in our pocket that makes us bolder.

Through prayer, common sense, and the power and authority of the holy spirit in us, we are already equipped to face—and conquer—what we are terrified of. Brothers and sisters, it's time to step forward and be brave!

This Week's Prayer: God, thank You for equipping and empowering me to face fear! Thank You for giving me power, love, and sound-mindedness. Help me cast off the chains of fear in my life and live fully in the freedom of Your grace and glory. Amen.

DENSE FOG ADVISORY

Yahweh opens the eyes of the blind. Yahweh lifts up those
who are bowed down; Yahweh loves the righteous.
(Psalm 146:8)

WHILE ON A TRIP TO VISIT a friend one day, I
had my first encounter with driving through fog. It's
amazing how different the world feels when it's
wrapped in that damp gray shawl; it can create the

illusion of solitude on a bustling stretch of road. It turns the trees to giants emerging from the veil. It erases everything except the world a quarter-mile ahead of you. In theory, it's pretty, calming, and ethereal.

In reality, fog is actually pretty terrible.

Driving through it was a white-knuckle experience. I couldn't tell when other vehicles were coming up beside me, and some were difficult to distinguish up ahead. I realized that day, that there's a reason they delay schools and issue advisories for dense fog. It takes a lot of focus to drive in those conditions. And it got me thinking (once I was actually *out* of the fog and could focus on something other than "Please God, please God let that giant Silverado on my tail actually *see me*") how fog is so colloquially used nowadays.

Think back to the last time you just couldn't get your day off the ground. You walked around in a haze that six cups of coffee and a set of jumping jacks couldn't cure. Someone might've told you that you had *brain fog*. We also use that term liberally of that nasty, muffle-headed feeling we get before, during, and even after a bad headcold. It's like someone unravels your brain into floss, whips it through a cotton candy machine, and sticks it back in there all pastel, puffy, and absolutely no nutritional value whatsoever. The best you can manage is a zombie-like grunt when asked how you're feeling.

Spiritual fog can happen to us, too. Those are the times when it seems so difficult to pray, when operating the manifestations of the holy spirit is a titan effort. If asked to give some spiritual advice, we crack our jaws, let out a pitiful moan, and shuffle away.

Sometimes the reason for this fog is evident: the cold condensation of stress, fear, worry, or sin that keeps our focus off of God; sometimes it's less obvious. No matter what the cause, though, there's one solution to our problem.

Have you ever seen fog burn off under sunlight? It's a real sight to behold. Pockets of thick mist like clouds cupped in low-lying places slowly turn to tufts, thinning out, then they're gone. No matter how thick the fog may be, as the sun climbs, it shreds the mist and the light comes through.

There is a similar biblical principle expressed by the Psalmist in Psalm 119:130: "The revelation of Your words **brings light**."

Even when the spiritual fog is thick in our lives, the rising of the sun—the words of life—and of The *Son*—the bringer of *all* light—can strip away the pall and restore depth and clarity to our senses. When we pray, appeal to God, and strive for the light, we *will* find it.

We just have to keep on driving no matter the density of the fog. Eventually, as we keep our gaze focused on the rising sun and on the Son of God, the cloudiness burns away.

This Week's Prayer: God, thank You for Your Son's light shining through the fog. Thank You for bringing clarity no matter how clouded things get. Please help me to continually seek You regardless of how difficult it is to see ahead! Amen.

WE MOLD TO OUR ENVIRONMENT

And do not be conformed to the pattern of this age, but be
transformed by the renewing of your mind...
(Romans 12:2)

FOR AS LONG AS I CAN remember, my mom
made it a point to get her bangs trimmed every six
weeks or so. But ask any woman who's had bangs
before, and she'll probably tell you they're a pain to

style. Unless you want to run around rocking the sheepdog look 24/7, you'd better get used to spending a good amount of time every morning taming those little wisps. My mom's no exception, but she's also a problem-solver. Years ago, she discovered that the best way to keep her bangs out of her eyes was with the convenient use of sunglasses. Wielded like a plastic headband, she keeps them on top of her head most of the time, scrunching her bangs down until she needs to drive in the sunlight. A perfect solution, really—but over time she realized the divot of the glasses was actually leaving a groove on the top of her head! We found it hilarious—and amazing—how something as insignificant as a lightweight pair of sunglasses on the top of her head could actually change the shape of the skull beneath.

Human beings are all made up of flesh and bone, and we mold to our environment. This sometimes happens gradually, like it did with my mom's head—but inevitably, it *does* happen. That's why God impresses on us over and over that we should carefully choose the company we keep and the things we let into our environment. These things shape us over time, sometimes so slowly we don't notice that instead of shaping *up*, we're becoming *misshapen.*

If you spend a lot of time with one person, you might notice that your behavior begins to mirror theirs!

Or if you marathon a TV show, or watch the same movie over and over again, you might start to reflect the mannerisms of certain characters. This is simply a result of the human penchant to craft ourselves after our environment. God points out the depth of this tendency when He says that *bad company corrupts good morals.*

The truth is, no matter how independent and self-realized we think we are, we all mold to fit our environment over time. That's important to keep in mind, because it's up to each of us to ensure that what we take in is edifying, true, virtuous, and uplifting; that the people we choose to surround ourselves with are encouraging us to behave well, not badly; and that when we start to shift, it's a godly change, molding us to be more like Christ.

This Week's Prayer: God, please help me to be aware of my environment. Give me the sensitivity to know if I'm molding myself to something that doesn't honor You. And please give me the strength to walk away from those environments so I can dwell more fully with You! Amen

THE MAN WHO WOULDN'T BE KING

The soul of Jonathan was bound together with the soul of David, and Jonathan loved him as his own soul.
(1 Samuel 18:1)

MOST PEOPLE HAVE A FAVORITE FIGURE from the Bible who they love reading about. For some, it's the life and lessons of Paul; others can't get enough of David's psalms, Joseph's rags-to-riches journey, Daniel's powerful witness, or Peter's relatable stubbornness. Of course, we all love reading about Jesus! And for me, especially reading the Bible from a very young age, one of my absolute favorite figures has always been Jonathan.

Comparatively speaking, we don't know a lot about Jonathan. We know he was Saul's son, one of the heirs to the throne; we know he was probably married, because he had a son, an heir of his own; and we know he was an invaluable friend to David. I think that's what always drew me toward their story: the Bible cuts no corners in making it clear that David and Jonathan loved each other like brothers, just like I love *my* brother.

But Jonathan wasn't only a shining example of a godly, loving friend; he was also an example of how, under any circumstances, a person can accept and embrace God's plan with absolute humility. Check out the story of David's ascension to the throne:

So, first, we have Saul, who's king...and, let's be frank, he's not a very good one. Even when he's leading his men on military strikes, his blunders and flashes of cowardice are costing Israel a lot. And then you have Jonathan, the prince, who takes his armor-bearer, leaves camp in the dead of night, and slaughters twenty Philistines, putting the rest of them in a frenzy. By military standards, Jonathan was a pretty cool guy—the kind you'd want to have in line for the throne. Which he was.

Then along comes David. God's anointed one. The Man Who Will Be King. David is in close quarters with Saul pretty often after that whole Goliath incident, where David did Saul a *serious* favor. If you follow the biblical record, David continues to gain rank and favor in the eyes of the people, becoming a musician and a military man, and even marrying Saul's daughter. He's practically moving into Saul's house! At this point, it becomes more and more clear that David has God's favor as well as the people's, and we see Saul consumed by jealousy...eaten alive by it. He isn't a fool; he knows this shepherd boy is going to take his throne someday.

Saul's opinion of David soured pretty quickly after that, and a lot has been said about the contention between them—almost a cat-and-mouse game carried out over the years as David fled and Saul pursued. Not a lot gets said about Jonathan during all of this, other than the time when he helped David discover Saul's murderous intent on his life and then sent him away.

But think about it this way: Saul was king, but Jonathan was a *prince*. If he was the eldest, he might've even been *next* in line for the throne. That was a big deal, especially when he was the son of Israel's very first king. He'd likely been groomed for royalty for many, many years. So when David showed up on the scene, Jonathan had every opportunity to indulge in the same blind fury as his father; he could've campaigned with Saul against David, deceived him with an imitation of friendship, or fought him outright for the throne the same way David's own sons squabbled for rights to rulership years later.

But the powerful testimony of Jonathan's life was that he did none of those things. He may as well have stripped off his sword and laid it at David's feet. He saw the ordination of God on David's life and rather than fighting against it the way Saul did, Jonathan—a prince of Israel—embraced David's calling. He welcomed him as king and brother, forging a fast friendship that, following Jonathan's death, David declared was "more wonderful than the love of women."

Jonathan loved David with an unselfish, unpretentious, fearless brotherly love that had no strings attached. Jonathan helped David escape Saul's wrath, lied to Saul's face about it, and nearly lost his head because of that, all for God's chosen king.

How often do we stand in the same place as Jonathan? How often do we think we're owed something, that we deserve something, and then we lose it? I know I don't tend to be a graceful loser when it comes down to it...and I'm never deprived of something as monumental as the potential future throne of an entire nation.

But the plans of the Father don't always end with us coming out in the spotlight, and Jonathan set an amazing example when the spotlight passed away from him. On the one hand, he saw what his father was doing to David; on the other, he saw God's plan for David's life. And then he followed that plan, trusting that God knew best with whoever He chose for that throne.

Understanding the truth of Jonathan's life, his acceptance of God's plans, and even the role he played in helping David survive and take the throne, is a powerful lesson. Sometimes we have to secede the things we want—even the things we think we deserve— because God's will is going in a different direction. And like Jonathan—the prince who would never become king—we have a choice. We can rebel against God's way and see how far that gets us...or we can embrace the ordination of the Creator, place ourselves wholeheartedly in His footsteps, and bind ourselves to His purposes with a selfless, consuming love.

This Week's Prayer: God, thank You for the examples You give in Your Word for the kind of person I can be! Please help me to be someone who, like Jonathan, lays aside what I think I'm owed or deserve so I can follow Your plans wholeheartedly. Amen.

WHO SITS ON THE THRONE?

Yahweh has established his throne in the heavens, and his
kingdom rules over all.
(Psalm 103:19)

THRONES ARE POWERFUL SYMBOLS. THEY have long stood to represent the seat of power for kings, even substituted as a direct reference for that power or the one who holds it. Thrones are referenced throughout the Bible to establish an image of enduring political might, the fortitude of generations, the majesty and splendor of those in power, and the influence wielded by families so long as they followed God's leading.

Even in a modern day and age, and particularly in Western culture where the closest most come to sitting on a throne is the euphemistic reference to the toilet, the symbolism is hardly absent. One of the most popular shows and book series of our time is called *Game of Thrones*, and the most famous photo from it is of—what else?—an enormous, weapon-studded throne, a symbol of incredible influence in the books.

One thing that's universally understood about the throne is that it's where the king sits. It's not just a chair, it's a seat of power. Royalty and nobility inhabit these places in every kingdom, and conquering kings sat on the thrones of those they supplanted. As Psalms reiterates many times, there is an enduring, heavenly throne where God sits. There is also a throne established for Christ, *the* King of Kings, which prophesied to be established forever and ever way back in Psalm 101. Another Psalmist used the analogy of a throne "hurled to the ground" to emphasize the utter breaking apart of his enemy's power by God.

One day I found a note on my mom's desk that really got me thinking about these seats of power. It was just one simple question: *Who sits on the throne of your heart?*

Our bodies are small kingdoms. We govern them day-to-day, deciding how we nourish, upkeep, and dispatch them. But in the center of each kingdom is the heart—and no matter what, something always sits on the throne of our hearts. When we accept Jesus as Lord, we make an ongoing commitment to enthrone him on this noble seat; but this can be a struggle to maintain, because other things are always warring for our affection, our attention, and the ultimate seat of power in our lives. Insidious idolatry can slip in, stealing the King's throne without us even noticing.

The warfare to reclaim the throne of our hearts for Christ is a lifelong battle that becomes easier to fight once we are truly conscious of it. Who are we serving? What is the focus of our attention, the thing or the "someone" we turn to in times of turmoil? When we take the time to look at the throne inside our kingdom, to take stock of who sits on it, we may be forced to confront the fact that something else had crept up the steps and into the chair.

It's up to us to reclaim the throne in the name of the Rightful King whose flag we fight under. There isn't any end to this struggle while we have an Enemy whose goal from the onset has been to sit the most powerful throne in the world: the one at the top of God's holy mountain. He can't have that, of course, so he'll settle for slipping things onto the thrones inside us that don't belong there—the kings of pride, ambition, selfishness, addiction, and so many more—to distract and derail the calling God has placed on each of our lives.

Luckily, when we step into the battle to keep our hearts pure and our focus where it belongs—on our mighty King—it's a fight we don't face alone. The conquering King of Kings wages war beside us, and the storms become easier to weather, the right thing easier to do, and the race easier to run when we take the time to make sure that the rightful King sits on the throne in our hearts. It's him we serve...and it's him, and him alone, to whom we bend the knee.

This Week's Prayer: God, thank You for Your Son, who is King of Kings and Lord of Lords! Jesus, I surrender the throne of my heart to you. Help me not to let anyone or anything else take that seat! Amen.

LOOKING THROUGH THE KEYHOLE

There are also many other things that Jesus did, which if
every one of them were written down, I suppose that even the
world itself could not contain the books that would be written.
(John 21:25)

ONE OF THE LANDMARK ATTRACTIONS IN
the United States is the Library of Congress. Located
in our nation's capital, it sports the title of "the library

with the most books *in the world*"—more than 36 million by some estimates.

Imagine the undertaking it would be to read them all! If you could devote eight hours a day to reading, at 250 words per minute, you could manage about 120,000 words a day. And there are roughly 2,304,000,000,000 words in the Library of Congress. So, yeah...that's about 2,190 years or nearly 2.2 millennia of reading.

It goes without saying that even the most avid reader of all time wouldn't be able to cover the entire scope of material in the Library of Congress in their lifetime. The library itself is enormous, housing 838 miles of shelves within its walls. Some brilliant architects certainly had their hands in the mix to ensure that one library could house so many words—words of fiction and history, religion and science, in multiple languages with their origins spanning across thousands of years.

I could talk about books and libraries like this all day. There was a pretty important historical figure who had something to say about books, too: the Apostle John. Referring to the Rabbi he followed, John had this to say as the parting word of his Gospel:

John 21:25

And there are also many other things that Jesus did, which if every one of them were written down, I suppose that even the world itself could not contain the   books   that   would   be   written.

Stop and think about that for a second. Really take it in.

We have four Gospels, many times covering the same events from different points of view, all painting the picture of the perfect Christ, the suffering servant and conquering king, the hero of all mankind. And yet what we see Jesus do—the infirm that he mended, the sick he healed, the dead he raised, the demons he cast out, the restoration of mankind that he accomplished, all of it—is like looking through a keyhole into a small sliver of a life that was beyond our comprehension.

One infinitesimal library on a few city lots in the heart of Washington, D.C. houses more books than one person can read in their lifetime; and yet John was inspired by God to write that the things Jesus did could fill up more books than *the entire world could contain.*

Just think of the stories about Jesus that you *haven't* heard. The miracles, the wonders, the life-altering acts he performed. And that same Jesus is still working powerfully behind the scenes on behalf of those he loves.

Two thousand years ago, Jesus had already done enough in this world that it couldn't contain all the records of his actions. Now imagine the stories Jesus will have to tell when we see him face-to-face one day— the accounts of his powerful works, the spiritual warfare, the miracles and interventions taking place over thousands of years. It's almost incomprehensible, and I can only say one thing for certain: we're definitely going to need a bigger library!

This Week's Prayer: God, thank You for the tremendous, awe-inspiring life of Your Son! Please help me to always be mindful of his powerful words and deeds, and help me represent him, and You, honorably to the world. Amen.

GETTING UNTANGLED

"Ask, and it will be given to you; seek, and you will find;
knock, and it will be opened to you.
(Matthew 7:7)

BEFORE WIRELESS HEADPHONES REALLY BECAME a thing, people out and about in public had no choice but to listen to music with corded headphones tethering them to their musical devices.

Many a phone and MP3 player saw its bitter, cracked-screen demise at the end of a hapless fall as the listener stepped away from the device too quickly or the headphones got hung up on something and the tug of the cords pulled the player off its safe resting place.

One thing that every corded-headphone user knows and hates is just how notorious these little things are for getting hopelessly tangled while in one's purse, pocket, or backpack. The internet abounds with comics poking fun at how you can tuck away your headphones, perfectly wrapped and tied off, only to pull them back out looking like Medusa's snarling dreadlocks on a bad hair day.

This anomaly of self-tangling headphones is one I am sadly all-too familiar with...in fact, it's a running joke between my husband and me. When we were still just engaged, he came up to me one day in a fit of laughter carrying a little surprise: he'd cut out a comic panel of a little girl sitting in her bed, holding a pair of perfectly disentangled headphones as she triumphantly declared, "Hooray! The headphone fairy fixed my headphones last night!" And the jokester had written *my* name across the girl's shirt.

Years later, I still laugh at this comic every time I see it hanging on our fridge, but sometimes I feel it says a lot more about me than just my propensity for snarled headphones.

In truth, my life's a lot like a headphone cord: whenever I think I've got everything perfectly wrapped up and neatly tucked where it belongs, that's usually when things are entwining hopelessly under the surface. When I look again, I find they really weren't as perfect, fixed, or healed as I thought.

At that point, more often than not, I come to grips with the fact that I don't stand a chance of getting things unknotted on my own...at least, not without running the risk of seriously damaging my inner wiring.

So then I remind myself that I have Someone—not a headphone fairy, but my Heavenly Father—Who excels at unknotting the messes, even the ones I make by pretending everything's cool and I've got it under control. Rather than trying (and failing!) to keep these struggles, personal issues, and weaknesses from getting tangled, what I need to do is bring them to the Great Detangler for help.

If you're struggling with some knotted cords that keep getting scrambled no matter how many times you've tried to smooth them out, I deeply encourage you to take your problems to the Great Detangler, too. His methods help us to really get those knots out...and in a way that prevents them from ever getting tangled again.

Most of us would be overjoyed to have that solution for our headphone cords...why not with our life struggles, too?

This Week's Prayer: God, thank You for being a Great Detangler! Thank You that no matter how messy and tangled up my life gets, You faithfully set things straight when I turn to You. Please help me to be mindful of this and always come running to You first when things start to get tangled. Amen.

GOD'S LEMONADE STAND

In everything by prayer and supplication with
thanksgiving let your requests be made known to God.
(Philippians 4:6)

ONCE UPON A TIME, GOD started a lemonade
stand unlike any other: you bring the lemons, and He
makes the lemonade.

Contrary to what is often expressed in Christian circles, God is not responsible for all the terrible things that happen in this world. Tornadoes and floods, miscarriages and illnesses, deaths and disasters aren't the result of some cosmic joke played by a Creator growing bored after an infinity of overseeing the universe. It would take so much time to cover all the evidence of how God is not responsible for the sufferings of mankind, so a better question to address right now might be: what does God *do* about suffering?

This is where the lemonade comes into play.

Imagine that the sufferings we face are lemons. They're the result of the freewill choices made by us and others; they're the fruit of living in a fallen world; they're the mutated byproducts of the mass manipulation caused by of the god of this age, the Serpent who is the true source of the sickness, suffering, and death we see around us. By no means are they plucked from the Tree of Life...but here we have them anyway, a bushel full of sour citrus sufferings. So what do we do with them?

One of the most powerful ways we can face our tribulations in this dark age is to bring them in prayer to God. This is akin to taking our lemons to God's lemonade stand and saying, "Here's what I've got. Can You make something of it?" This requires more from us than merely dwelling in our woes...we take an active role. We acknowledge that something is wrong, and we ask Someone greater than us to show us what can be done about it.

Especially when we're knee-deep in the sheer awfulness that comes with living in a cursed world, it can be difficult to see how our trials can be made into something sweet. There doesn't seem to be enough spiritual sugar to mend a cancer diagnosis, the death of a loved one, or the loss of a much-needed job.

But that's the beauty of serving a Creator who sees so much farther than our mortal gaze can reach. When we take our mourning to God, He can turn it to dancing (Psalm 30:11). He can deliver the body from illness; He can mend broken spirits, broken bodies, and broken hearts. He can bring a friend along to remind us that we don't face our struggles alone. When the unseen circumstances in the physical and spiritual realms prevent a miraculous turnaround in our circumstances, we have a God who sits beside us on the sidewalk in the pouring rain and grieves with us. And we have a God who, through it all, is inarguably and untiringly working for the good of those who love Him (Romans 8:28).

Sometimes God requires more of us than we may expect to move mountains in our own lives. It can be difficult, stressful, sometimes downright unpleasant even just to walk out a trial and wait for the rainbow after the rain. Doing work for a perfect One when we ourselves are imperfect isn't always enjoyable, and it often requires waiting for His timing when our impatient hands want to wrap around a solution *right now*.

We see our circumstances of the moment and panic; God sees the whole matter and says, "I've got you." And sometimes the only thing we can do is lash ourselves to the mast, ride out the waves, and praise God in the storm.

But no matter what trials we face, it never hurts to say a prayer, take our lemons to God, and trust Him to make them into lemonade.

This Week's Prayer: God, thank You for Your overwhelming power that can turn even the worst circumstances to good! Please help me to always be mindful of how You care for me even when I feel lost, alone, attacked or adrift. May I never lose sight of Your love! Amen.

HOW DO I BRING CHRIST TO PEOPLE?

Go and make disciples of all the nations, baptizing them in
the name of the Father and the Son and the holy spirit...
(Matthew 28:19)

EVEN AFTER WE DECIDE TO make the effort to
"bring people to Christ," the question that stalls many
Christians is, "How do I actually do this?" There are

plenty of resources that will tell you how to witness, from door-to-door evangelism to engaging with the people you sit next to on a plane...not all of which are bad, but not all of which work, either.

Maybe a better question is, "How do I bring *Christ* to people?"

Jesus is the hero in a story written for the ages. He's the one who swooped in and saved folks from the suffocating, heavy laws of the religious leadership. He was the crusader of the underprivileged, the voice of reason in a maelstrom of chaos that continues to this day. How could I *not* want to emulate him? How could I *not* want to speak of him like the awesome victor he is, the champion of the most profound epic of all time?

So often, we burden Jesus with the constraints of paradigms, frame him in the outline of our own understanding, or try to fit him in the box of our position—and no matter if our position is really "right" or not, we can still complicate the Good News of Jesus Christ with it. In order to be Jesus's ambassadors, we have to represent him the way he truly was back when he walked the earth, without two thousand years of opinions foisted on his shoulders.

The truth is, sometimes the voice of Jesus speaks, not in the citation of a chapter and verse, but in a gentle admonition. In the godly advice that reaps a good outcome. In the leap of trust that profits greatly. In the closeness of a perfect man who loved a leper the world pulled away from; who said "Your sins are forgiven"; who insisted he'd come for the sick, not the healthy.

One of the best ways we emulate Jesus is through love. Love is hardwired into us, built into our hearts and souls, our very bones. Sometimes doctrine, religion, and our own ideas of right and wrong can shackle our ability to portray Jesus in the barrier-breaking, earth-shattering, revolutionary way that he *was* and *is*: loving with no holds barred. Loving the sick, the broken, the degenerate. Loving people out of sin and into repentance. Loving to the point of pain—loving beyond what physical limits the human body can endure.

In order to be like him, we must push ourselves. We must love radically. We must show them Jesus through our ability to love in a world that tells us to put ourselves first, look out for number one, and take care of our own needs above all others.

The message of Jesus should live in everything we do. Not like a cartoon skit where we're whispering over a secret, hoping people will crowd around us asking what we're so interested in, but living it openly, weaving our love of Jesus into every choice we make, every step we take, so that the joy of the Lord stands as our undeniable witness.

Whether or not people come to Jesus isn't up to us. It's between him and the individual. But what we can do is bring *Christ* to *people*.

Our whole lives are a testimony of the one we serve, a reflection of the man Jesus was, is, and will always be. More often than we know, it's not our words that will show people the light of Jesus's love in us—it's our actions.

What kind of story will yours tell?

This Week's Prayer: Jesus, thank you for your ministry and sacrifice! Please help me to live as a worthy witness and ambassador for you. May I honor you always in how I bring the good news about you to people both in word and deed. Amen.

FEEL THE BURN

Let us also run with endurance the race that is set before us...
(Hebrews 12:1)

I'VE FOUND MYSELF REFLECTING A lot on a conversation I once had with a sibling in Christ. We were on the subject of "unsavory thoughts" and how insidious they are—how difficult it is to get ahead of them. After a lot of banter about the subject, I reminded my friend that no matter how overwhelming those thoughts seem, we can still lead them captive in obedience to Christ.

"I know the Bible *says* that," my friend complained, "but I don't think I can do that. It's just so hard!"

Well, yeah, I remember thinking, but since when does that mean it *can't* be done?

Where in the world did we get this idea that something is "right" or "from God" only if it's *easy*? How many people have chosen to walk away from their relationship with God because one of His commands, His requirements for a godly life, was too hard? And then some have assumed that if God was real, He would never ask them to do something so difficult—Q.E.D., God must not be real.

A lot of mainstream Christianity—in an effort, I suspect, to draw more converts—has defined the Christian walk as a health-and-wealth package. If you swear your fealty to Christ, it's nothing but sweet benefits for the rest of forever.

But that's not really true, is it? We're the same broken people after we come to Christ as we were before. With his help, thankfully, we have a means to truly repair that brokenness; but it's a long road, and for the most part, it's not easy. Convicted, transformed, and now ushered toward the light, we have to fight those insidious thoughts, those sinful impulses, every step of the way. And it's *not* easy. In fact, the Apostle Paul compares doing the work of the Lord to running a race.

Full confession: I am not a race-runner. I am not a sprinter. I don't even run to my mailbox. Running and I aren't buddies. But I do have several friends who are passionate runners, and one thing I've gleaned from conversations with them is that, even when you LOVE to do it, running is not *easy*. Are there things you can do to make it *easier*? Totally! Getting in shape, staying fit, eating well, and training are just a few things that help peak performance.

But even when they're in their prime, many runners say that somewhere along the racecourse—whether it's the first, second, fifth, or fifteenth mile—it starts to get *hard*. The lungs and legs are burning, all those muscles are taxed and tired, and you might just want to sit down or at least walk all the way to the end of the race.

But that's not what the race is about. Runners don't run because it's *easy*. They run because on some level, they have the *passion to do it*.

Our spiritual journey is the same way. People like to call it a spiritual "walk." It's not. It's a spiritual "RUN." It's a race—not against the other runners, but against ourselves. To reach the finish line without giving up requires perseverance. It demands that we *push through the burn*.

Will this be easy? No way! Are there things we can do to make it *easier*? You bet! Staying active in prayer, keeping our lives in shape with Scripture, feeding our hearts and minds with good company...these are all things that make the race easier. But the race is still a race. God did not call us to run it because it was the easy thing to do, but because it's the *right race to run.*

For that reason, we can't allow ourselves to sink into that quitter's mindset of taking the easy road. Our racecourse does not run that way. It goes over hills and into valleys and up and down mountains. It takes us to breathtaking heights we would never achieve otherwise. It's not an easy course to run, but I promise you, it will always be worth the burn.

This Week's Prayer: God, thank You for equipping me to run this race for You! Please strengthen me and bolster my endurance so I may run it well, pleasing and honoring You! Amen.

FOUR WAYS TO REVIVE A
FELLOWSHIP

**And they devoted themselves to the apostles' teaching, and
to fellowship, to the breaking of bread, and to prayer.
(Acts 2:42)**

FOR AS FAR BACK AS I can remember in my
childhood, we always ran a Tuesday night Bible
study out of our home. I was younger than five when
we started this tradition, and the weekly meeting,

which we called "Tuesday Night Fellowship," continued until I was about fourteen/fifteen. That's quite a few Tuesdays! Couple in the holiday parties, cookouts, and other celebrations, and the core families all spent quite a bit of time together.

Inevitably, there were periods of time where our fellowship sort of...stagnated. It involved the same meal, teaching, and playtime for us kids, week after week. So the adults often tried to find ways to rock the boat and make fellowship interesting and exciting again. Some of what we tried really worked! Some of it didn't. But as I've gotten older, one thing I've learned is that most home churches, Bible studies, and fellowships seem to go through phases where things become repetitive and unengaging.

As I've observed what these fellowships do to try and breathe a sense of vitality back into their gathering, there are a few I've noticed that keep cropping up because they're pretty successful! So whether you're stagnating, just starting a fellowship, or trying to stay ahead of a burnout, here are four things you can try in order to "shake up" the monotony that sometimes paralyzes a home fellowship:

1. Hold a Q&A

If your fellowship is anything like ours was, you probably have one person at a time, one week at a time, sharing what's currently inspiring or motivating them. This can become disengaging for the rest of the fellowship because what's crucial for one person (the teacher) might not have as big an impact on others (the hearers)—so the people walk away not feeling spiritually "fed".

Instead of having a teacher present what's inspiring for just him/her, consider holding a Q&A session. Have your fellowship write down on a slip of paper or an index card one question about a biblical topic that's weighing on their hearts. Then devote the next meeting to tackling one, or several, or ALL of those questions! This allows the people who aren't teaching to actively engage because they have a personal stake in what's being taught.

You can also spread out the questions through multiple meetings, depending on the size of your fellowship. Encourage people not to be afraid to ask the tough questions, the uncomfortable or difficult ones; these often create a crucible, and crucibles refine us and help us grow.

2. Have A Prayer Night

When I was a kid, we had a rocking chair that took up the middle of the living room—mostly because it was our video game chair and we couldn't be bothered to move it from in front of the TV every Tuesday. But we adapted that chair into what my parents called "the hot seat." Almost every week someone had a struggle that needed praying for. Something was weighing them down, and that landed them in "the hot seat," where we'd all circle around the person in the rocking chair and pray fervently over them.

Throughout the course of our fellowship, I remember several times when all we did was circle up and pray. When a friend relapsed with cancer; when 9/11 happened; when there was hurt or anger or illness in our midst. Teachings are wonderful and sharings have their place, but if your fellowship is feeling detached, disassociated, or weighed down with life's struggles, consider holding an exclusive "prayer night." Bring everyone together and simply pray over every little (or big!) thing that's bothering each of you.

Not only is this a powerful form of spiritual warfare, but it can also knit your fellowship together in the bonds of unity as you fight for one another and bring your requests together before God.

3. Start A Series

Another problem some fellowships run into is a feeling as if the same topics are being covered over and over again, and usually by the same people. There's nothing necessarily wrong with that, but repetition isn't the only way we absorb information; sometimes we need to see things in a new light. It's also important that we expand our spiritual horizons so we can continue to grow and mature.

In the same vein as the Q&A session, taking on a series taught by a different teacher can add a unique flavor to your fellowship. If there's a particular subject you're interested in, consider finding an audio, YouTube, or video seminar that covers it.

Research defending the Faith, or Christian persecution; dive into the history of Christianity; do a focus group for women, men, couples, parents, etc. find something that appeals to your fellowship and take that journey together. This can often open the door to deep discussion as everyone walks that road of discovery side-by-side.

4. Eat A Meal Together

Some fellowships try to make the community meal a part of every meeting. But there are others who just show up, listen up, get up, and leave. If your fellowship falls into the second category, consider trying to host a meal together; have everyone pitch in and bring a dish, and sit down to eat together with no distractions.

This was a habit that the apostles encouraged...so much so, in fact, that it's considered part of their "creed" in Acts 2! Breaking bread is something that families have done together since ancient times, and I can attest from experience that sharing a meal with your fellowship does create a sense of family. You become privy to one another's struggles, day-to-day lives, and unique intricacies as you banter over a bowl of soup or a good burger. That kind of intimacy doesn't always come to light with small talk before or after a teaching.

Some of the best memories are made and the best times are had over a good meal...this is as true for fellowships as for families.

Conclusion

There are so many ways that we can shake up and breathe life back into our fellowships when things get stale. If you feel like your fellowship is growing lax with the same ol' same ol' every meeting, consider trying out one of the tactics above!

This Week's Prayer: God, thank You for creating us for relationship! Please bless and protect all those who gather in Your name. And please help me to make the most of my own fellowship experience. Amen.

LET DADDY FIX IT!

And after you have suffered a little while, the God of all grace [...] will himself restore, confirm, strengthen, and establish you.
(1 Peter 5:10)

GOD KNEW WHAT HE WAS doing when He named Himself the *Father* to all those who believe and are saved. A healthy, godly relationship between father and child is one of the most precious bonds I've ever witnessed; and I can't believe the lessons I've learned about God, and our relationship with Him as His children, from watching my friends' kids interact with their dads and my own son interact with his daddy.

One example that stands out to me is a time when my mom and I were babysitting for family friends. My mom was wearing a bangle designed with about an inch-wide opening between the halves. Partway through the night, one of the kids crawled into her lap and noticed for the first time that the bangle wouldn't clasp. In her young mind, that screamed one word: *BROKEN*.

"Oh no, it broken!" she declared with her tiny lisp. Despite our reassurances, she wouldn't believe it was made that way, and instead patted my mom's wrist while reassuring her, "We fix it when Daddy come home. Daddy fix *anything*."

So much childlike faith! In almost three years of life, this little girl had not yet encountered any scenario where Daddy couldn't make everything better. That of course changed as she grew up, which is a normal, healthy part of life; if we all still needed our dads to come change a lightbulb for us when we're thirty-five, chances are we missed a maturity step.

But *independence* seems to have become, not just a byproduct of growing up, but actually the ultimate *goal*.

The need to not need *anything* or *anyone* is paramount to almost every achievement for young adults especially. But when it comes to God—our *Heavenly Dad*—independence from Him only breeds isolation, loneliness, and pain. It leaves us trying to solve problems on our own that are too big for us; and yet the world implies, often in subtle, sneaky ways, that needing Daddy to fix something is weakness.

I've struggled with this for years...in fact, I still struggle sometimes to pray for things, feeling as if I'm showing weakness if I have to take it to God rather than handling it myself. But hearing the innocent perspective of that little girl started a change in me. In the years since, I've found myself wanting to cleave to God with as much absolute trust as my friend's daughter had in her daddy that night. I want to believe that *whatever* is broken, I can take it to God and He'll find a way to mend it. I want my first thought, my gut-reaction to be, "Let's take it to God. I know He can handle this."

The trust of a daughter in the mountains her Father can move. The absolute belief that not only *can* He, but He *will*. That's the confidence, the adoration, the childlike faith that brings us peace in every circumstance—and that brings us closer to God.

So whatever may be going on in your life, whatever brokenness you're facing, I encourage you to take it to our Heavenly Father. He can fix *anything*.

This Week's Prayer: God, thank You for being such a fixer of all things! Help me to always be mindful to bring the broken things in my life to You so You can work Your power in every situation and bring about good! Amen.

THE IMITATION OF INTIMACY

Now I know only in part, but then I will know fully just as
also I was fully known.
(1 Corinthians 13:12)

WHEN I WAS IN SIXTH GRADE, the only year I
was public-schooled, I made my first "neighborhood
friend," Kay. We spent the summer between our
sixth and seventh grade years biking the six or so

blocks to each other's houses, peeling ourselves out of bed at the crack of dawn to fish for crawdads in the storm culvert, and getting slushies, hot dogs, and candy from the local gas station or Dog n' Suds.

At the time, I thought my friendship with Kay was pure magic. One of my favorite things about her was the wild stories she told about her grandparents' Montana farm where the wolves howled at dawn and dusk, and about her pet horse, Star, who was boarded at some fancy stable outside the city. These stories were awe-inspiring, especially considering the negligent parents she always wanted to get away from, the derelict state of her house, and the fact that we were both from a neighborhood that was rapidly becoming "lower middle class" by the time Kay moved there.

It wasn't until summer passed away that I learned about some contradicting stories Kay had told to mutual acquaintances. I started to awaken from my bedazzlement and faced a hard truth: Kay had been lying for most of the summer. There was no horse and no Montana farm; she'd admitted that to some of our other friends.

The more I thought about it, the more I realized that our friendship had been built on lie after lie, most of which made Kay seem more fortunate than she really was. This revelation drove a wedge between us; Kay couldn't bring herself to admit to my face that these stories were a lie, and I couldn't fathom being friends with someone who always lied to me. We drifted apart soon after, but it wasn't until over a decade later that I realized there was a phrase for what Kay and I really shared that summer: an *imitation of intimacy.*

Sure, we'd had fun together...but had we ever really been close? How could we call ourselves friends when most of the things she told me about herself were lies?

I think this imitational relationship happens more often than we know; not always in full-blown lies like I experienced with Kay, but often in subtler ways. Have you ever had a friend that you white-lied to, trying to endear yourself to them in whatever way you thought they *wanted* you to? Have you ever finessed the details of your career or degree to make it seem a little more appealing to a certain circle of acquaintances? Have you ever been in a relationship where you just went along with whatever your significant other wanted because you felt that would bring you closer together?

In cases like these, we're not really being true to ourselves, expressing our hearts, or having what the Greeks would call *koinonia* (full sharing). Instead, we are baring a sliver of ourselves and masquerading the rest, imitating the true intimacy of a trusting relationship in order to have approval or at least not rock the boat.

Sadly, the imitation of intimacy is not relegated to how people interact with each other...it has its fingers in the spiritual realm, too. Growing up, I crossed paths with so many people who prayed deep, powerful prayers in church and fellowship, then turned around and lashed out in anger toward their families, indulged in substance abuse, or engaged in sexual sin. These were all another imitation of intimacy: it wasn't that those people meant to be hypocritical, per se; they truly *longed* for closeness with God, but they saw themselves as unworthy, and the moment the prayers left their lips, they had already decided in their hearts that God wouldn't hear them. In anguish of that, they turned back to their sin to mask the hurt. And the bitter cycle continued.

So, what can we do to combat the imitation of intimacy in our lives? I believe one of the first things it to honestly admit to ourselves the areas in which we've settled for the imitation rather than the true intimacy. Consider:

- Have I resorted to casual flirting over lasting romance?
- Have I forsaken deep, personal friendships for shallow chit-chat about the best parts of my life?
- Have I lied or embellished to make myself seem more important?
- Have I gone along with something I didn't want to do for fear of being rejected if I spoke up?

- Have I let recitation from a Sunday pew replace a true relationship with God?

Once we identify the places in our lives where comfortable imitation has taken hold, then we can begin to break down whatever walls are keeping us wedged there. Whether it's a sense of unworthiness, fear of judgement, feelings of self-condemnation, guilt, grief, shame, regret, loss, panic...these can all be healed.

The depth of true intimacy begins when we recognize we can have an intimate relationship with our Heavenly Father, and when we fully embrace that opportunity. When we are no longer putting on airs with Him (useless, anyway—He sees everything, even straight through our facade), we can begin to draw our true sense of worth from His vast love. Through that love, which doesn't fail even at our darkest, we can attain healing in *whatever* area has stymied our ability to relate wholeheartedly with others—whether that's lies, acquiescence, addiction, or any other thing. And when we understand our value in the eyes of the One who created us, that's where we can begin to *fully share*, in all our relationships, the priceless uniqueness of who we are.

When we know that we are enough—worthy enough, valued enough, and loved by God despite however much we sin—so much of that fear of rejection, judgement, and condemnation can be resolved. This allows us to drop the imitation and truly engage. This sort of freedom and trust in God allows us to have full sharing with our friends, families, and significant others. It starts with God and branches out from there. And once we embrace true intimacy with the Maker of all Life, who formed and fashioned us, anything is possible.

This Week's Prayer: God, thank You for the opportunity to have intimate relationship with You and others! Please help me to engage in healthy full sharing with both You and Jesus, and those with whom it's safe in my life. Amen.

A CHANGE OF PLANS

God said to Jonah, "Is it right for you to be angry about the
vine?" He said, "I am right to be angry, even to death."
(Jonah 4:8b-9)

I AM WHAT MY FAMILY lovingly calls an
"administrative nerd." Organization is my passion;
and never have I liked when things go awry less
than when it interferes with not just my peace, but

the peace of those around me. Compounding compassion with organizational perfectionism can lead to one unpleasant morning, as was the case once when a hitch in a well-laid (and months old, might I add) plan left not only me, but friends and family, scrambling for a last-minute solution.

In the midst of the chaos—during that dreaded period where you've done all you can, and all that's left is to wait—I was silently fuming at my desk. This whole situation was so unfair, I found myself thinking. We'd had this plan in place for months, *months*, and *now*, a week before everything was set to kick off...*now* there's a change of plan? Why us, God, why us? I just want to shrink and disappear, I don't want to go through this, ARGH!

And then, one of those quiet thoughts: *Don't be a Jonah.*

Oh.

Of all the biblical figures, perhaps none stand so obstinately contrary to the sacrificial "not my will but yours be done" attitude of Jesus than our friend Jonah. I can't say I have any idea what Jonah's life was like before God sent him to Nineveh, but I'm willing to bet *his* administrative idea did not involve hopping onto a camel's back and riding into the jaws of the enemy (Nineveh being, by gentle terms, a nasty, no good, not-nice place).

So Jonah scampered off to port, hopped on a boat, tried to sail to Tarshish—in the opposite direction, by the way—and...well, most of us know the rest. Fast forward: Jonah is rescued from the belly of the sea creature, makes his way to Nineveh, does as God tells him...and the people turn! God spares them. And Jonah's reaction to this change in plan?

COMPLAIN.

Jonah leaves the city and sits to wait and see what God will do. God sends a plant to shelter him from the scorching sun (I have it on good authority from my mom, after a pilgrimage to Israel, that shade is hard to come by and more precious than gold under the baking Middle East heat); then God sends a worm to eat the plant. Jonah complains. He's going to faint, it would be better if he just died, grumble, grumble...

Man oh man, I don't want to be like Jonah! Changes in plans are usually an inconvenience to at least some degree, but if my kneejerk reaction is to grumble, complain, and bemoan my very existence, that's a fairly good barometer that my heart is in the wrong place. I'm not looking at the bigger picture; I'm not looking for solutions, or for ways to learn and grow from this. I'm stewing under that scorching east wind, waiting to faint. And I don't want to be like that!

Inconvenience is a part of life. Plans will change—and it may rock the boat so much we wish we could just shrivel up and disappear. But the next time something happens to interrupt my carefully laid plans, rather than being like Jonah, I'll try being like Jesus, who changed his course at a whisper from God and stayed sensitive to the doubts, the fears, and the needs of those around him:

Mark 6:48-51

Around three in the morning· [Jesus] came toward them walking on the sea **and wanted to pass by them.** When they saw Him walking on the sea, they thought it was a ghost and cried out; for they all saw Him and were terrified. Immediately He spoke with them and said, "Have courage! It is I. Don't be afraid." **Then He got into the boat with them,** and the wind ceased.

This Week's Prayer: God, when plans change, help me keep my peace! Help me look for the lesson. And help me always find a way to do Your will— even when there's a change of plan. Amen.

ON PURPOSE, FOR A PURPOSE

For we are his workmanship, created in Christ Jesus for
good works...
(Ephesians 2:10)

I READ A QUTOE ONCE THAT seemed like such an obvious truth in retrospect, yet I'd never considered it before. It went something like this: "If you had never existed, *nothing* would be the same.

Everywhere you've been, every person you've ever interacted with, would have a different life experience...just because you were not there."

Sometimes it can be hard not to feel insignificant, as if our lives are short, soft shouts into the endless macrocosm of eternity. And yet it's true that as objects of mass and energy—creatures of *matter*—we displace the world around us as we move. This is undeniable. And as with most things in life, the world around us is a reflection of God's greater design for all mankind.

There is a purpose in God's plan for all of creation, and you play an irreplaceable part in it. The eyes of the One who sees all things, see you as well...your individual importance, your significance as one of many priceless parts of the Body of Christ. You were made to matter, with gifts and talents that no one else can bring to God's family—and to the world. And that being the case, God's plan for the world would not be the same without *the part that you play in it.*

As famous Christian author Max Lucado said: "You were made *on* purpose, *for* a purpose."

You will never be expendable to God, and the calling you have in the Body of Christ is no less important than another's, whether or not it's a highly-visible role. God's desire for you is that you would seek and find a way to sow seeds with your heavenly gifts and callings to spread love and truth, to break shackles and shine light from the hilltops of a broken world.

The witness of every Christian's existence is that, like our Savior Jesus who fulfilled the ultimate plan for redemption, we too have a purpose and a direction. Our lives have intentionality; we were not made to be forgotten—our lives are remembered forever by the loving Father who fashioned us. We are warriors, we are the called, we are beloved, we are the Body of Christ...we are Jesus-followers. So let's show others that their lives have meaning, too, bringing them to the only place where they can experience their true worth and calling: in the plan of the Creator who made *them* on purpose, for a purpose.

This Week's Prayer: God, thank You for creating me for a purpose! Thank you for placing a calling on my life. Please help me to fulfill it and serve You well! Amen.

GOD UNDERSTANDS *YOU*!

*But even all the hairs of your head have been counted. Do
not be afraid, you are of more value than many sparrows.*
(Luke 12:7)

ONE OF THE MOST FUNDAMENTAL cries of
the human spirit is to be heard and understood.
Unfortunately, there are so many things that put
barriers between us and other people:

miscommunication, misrepresentation, past hurts, the fear of rejection, the fear of being misunderstood, and on and on.

We may not bring our honest selves to a relationship because we are afraid of being mocked, misjudged, rejected, or abandoned. These fears can stem from a number of places, anywhere from unrecognized doubts to past experiences with unfavorable outcomes. When it comes down to it, connecting with others is just plain *hard*!

Nevertheless, connection is *why* we were created. In the very beginning of time as we know it, God created human beings because He desired a family of freewill beings, made in His image, with whom He could deeply and freely fellowship. That means that, like our Creator, we are made to connect in mutual, honest, *healthy* relationships, like what Jesus' followers experienced with him and each other.

We also need this kind of relationship with God. Unfortunately, this can be very hard for a *lot* of people.

As we more deeply grasp the magnitude of our great and awesome God, we find there are elements of reverence, awe, and maybe even a little fear that come along with it. If being in relationship with our fellow flawed humans is so intimidating, it's hard to even imagine having full-sharing with our flawless Heavenly Father. But that is exactly what He desires to cultivate with us.

I have known many people (and have even been this way myself) who have embraced the idea of a relationship with God, but then tried to keep certain parts of themselves out of the equation. They haven't wanted to show Him their brokenness for a host of reasons. But if we're really honest with ourselves, we must recognize that we can't keep the ugliness of our humanity out of God's sight. He sees it all, and He still wants to be in relationship with us—powerful, transformative, life-altering relationship!

Think about this, really let it soak in: *you cannot surprise God.* He already *gets* you—your best and worst qualities. At your proudest and your most humble. Your angriest and calmest. Your most sinful and most righteous moments are both before His eyes. You cannot surprise Him with your brokenness or uprightness.

So what God is asking of us is to enter into a relationship where we *don't try to hide*, because there is nothing we *can* hide. Our illusions are already stripped off, the darkness is exposed before we ever step into His presence. That's it. There's no need for posturing or false piety with Him.

Many people have someone they would consider their "best friend"—someone they feel comfortable exposing their deepest heart to, the good, the bad, and the ugly. I want you to really, deeply realize that *God is that "Someone" for every Christian.* Not only does He know us, but He *made* us. He loved us before we even chose to accept His offer for eternal life and enter into relationship with Him and His Son.

God is not holding you at arm's length. He is not shocked by your lowest lows. He welcomes you at your worst, and through Christ there is the opportunity for that "worst" to be transformed into your "best." Just reach out and take the hand of the One who *gets* you at your deepest core level...and let the relationship, the healing, the transformation, and the next step of the journey begin!

This Week's Prayer: God, thank You for understanding me and loving me so much! Please help me draw near to You at all times, knowing there are no walls between us. You know me and love me as I am and as You're leading me to be. Amen.

LEAVE THE 99

*If any man has 100 sheep, and one of them goes astray,
does he not leave the 99 on the mountains and seek the one
that went astray?*
(Matthew 18:12)

I'M A BIT OF AN Instagram fan. As a writer, the visual glimpses into other writers' routines really fascinates me. I was deeply blessed at one point by a fellow writer's Instagram post about leaning on God during tough times. But what really caught my eye about her post wasn't the content of the message so much as the picture that went along with it: a shot of her computer, with a sticker in the upper corner that caught my eye:

Leave the 99.

This sticker is a reference to the Parable of the Lost Sheep in Luke 15, where Jesus tells the religious leaders about how a man, having 100 sheep, would leave the 99 to find the one who was lost. So it is in heaven when one lost soul returns.

After seeing that sticker, what really stuck with me was one particular portion of that parable: "When he has found it, he joyfully puts it on his shoulders, and coming home, he calls his friends and neighbors together, saying to them, 'Rejoice with me, because I have found my lost sheep!'"

I deeply pondered the visual of that passage. A lost, wandering, tired sheep, carried on the shepherd's shoulders back to the flock; and the shepherd doesn't hide that sheep in the back of the flock, embarrassed by its foolish wandering. Instead, he gathers everyone close to rejoice over that sheep coming home. It's the redemption that's celebrated; it's never mentioned that the shepherd grumbles and curses the sheep as he climbs the hillsides in search of it.

I think our Good Shepherd feels the same about us. Even the most dedicated Jesus-follower is capable, and often guilty, of straying into sin. We may become lazy with our calling and set aside the things of God for the temptations of the world. Yet even when we are lost, Jesus relentlessly pursues us—each of us, as individuals. When the weariness and consequences of our wandering is finally too much and we run to him in earnest repentance of our sin, he carries us on his shoulders back to the flock.

Your Shepherd would leave the 99 to rescue you. He rejoices over your homecoming whenever you wander. How precious that love is...and how precious you are to him!

This Week's Prayer: Jesus, thank you for your miraculous and inspiring love! Thank you for leaving the 99 to come searching for ME when I go astray. May I never lose sight of how wonderous your love is—and how much I am loved by you and by God! Amen.

THE JOURNEY OF HOLINESS

Make them holy by the truth; your word is truth.
(John 17:17)

I'M SURE I'M NOT ALONE in wishing that giving my heart to Christ had resulted in an instant transformation into perfection. We're made in the image of God—who is spirit and holy—and we should be conformed to the image of Christ, who walked blamelessly before his Father. But following that example is so much easier said than done!

I used to think that if I could check off the list of "faith-behaviors," I would attain holiness. Luckily, as I've gotten older, I've learned to give grace to myself because true holiness is not a destination of perfection that I will ever reach in this life. I was born imperfect and will die that way. But I can still choose to live with *as much* holiness as possible.

There are three things that I've come to see as imperative to overcoming my own day-by-day struggle to walk a holy and upright life before my Lord. I hope these things are encouraging to you, too!

1. Be Formed by the Lord

Everyone and everything in this world has an agenda. It's good to recognize this and get it out of the way. Everything is pushing us either toward the Lord or away from him. And we have a choice about what we let into our arena...what we're willing to let shape us. Living a holy faith-journey requires the active decision to let God and Jesus form our hearts, and for their words and principles to be the ones that dictate our steps, rather than us being formed by a selfish, secular, or ungodly standard.

2. Be Transformed by the Renewing of Your Mind

No matter how badly we want to be in perfect standing with God, there is a daily tug-of-war on our minds...the ongoing struggle between our old and new natures. Because of this, our transformation—like holiness itself—is not a one-time thing, but a continuous renewal of our dedication to the Lord's leading in all areas where we may be tempted to behave sinfully. We are then able to do God's will in a more perfect, pleasing, and upright manner...a truly holy one, as He is holy.

3. Be Conformed to the Will of the Lord

Perhaps the most difficult part of living a holy life is to give up doing what appeals to us in order to do what is perfect and pleasing to the Lord. Rather than being conformed to the pattern of this world and this age, we must continuously conform ourselves to the standard God has set before us. Sometimes this is less of a day-to-day struggle and more of a minute-by-minute one. But once we surrender our hearts to be shaped by God's leading and submit to transformation, it becomes easier to follow His will rather than to remain enslaved to our own desires which are often selfish, wasteful, and not holy in the least.

The journey of holiness requires faithfulness to the Lord, death to self to become living sacrifices before

God, and the willpower and endurance to continue living in the cycle of submission, transformation, and conformation to God's will, over and over. It isn't an easy journey by any means; *arduous, grueling,* and *constant* are better words to describe it. But if our allegiance to the Lord is true, then so must our endeavors for holiness be. God and Jesus deserve absolutely *nothing less* from us.

This Week's Prayer: God, thank You for never abandoning or forsaking me on this journey toward holiness! Thank You for loving me every step of the way. Help me to live holier and more wholly for You, day by day. Amen.

A PRAYER FOR THE HEART OF GOD

**May your kingdom come! May your will be done on earth
as it is in heaven!
(Matthew 6:10)**

HAVE YOU EVER BEEN IN a situation where you just didn't know what to pray for *or* against?

There are times in our lives where the words of man bombard us constantly, obscuring the will of God. We can find ourselves torn between human ideals, uncertain of who is walking upright, who is deceived, if anyone is truly right or wrong, and most of all, how to conduct ourselves so that we are behaving in as Christlike a manner as possible. This can be especially difficult when we're uncertain if we are operating from a position of whole or partial facts! We want our prayers to be effective, but that in and of itself can be so difficult when we're not certain what we should even pray for.

While reflecting on the painful uncertainty that many people face when trying to navigate tricky and painful situations like these, I got to talking to God. I confessed to Him that I have often struggled with feelings of loss and bitterness when the words just wouldn't come, but that I never again want to be caught in a place where I feel too trapped to even pray. I asked Him to teach me what to say in those times when I don't know what to pray for.

And just like that, the words came to me—a prayer that my husband and I began to incorporate into our daily prayer time together. We've both found that when we feel lost or stuck, when words fail us as we face a problem and need help, discernment, and courage to navigate it, this prayer has brought us so much peace.

In time, I felt the pressure on my heart to share that simple, short, but heartfelt prayer with a wider community. It is my hope that this prayer will bring you the same sense of peace and direction as it has brought to my family, and that it will be helpful to you in times when words fail:

This Week's Prayer: Father God, give me eyes to see, ears to hear, and lips that speak YOUR truth— even if my voice shakes. Amen.

HOW'S *YOUR* WALK?

For we must all be exposed before the judgment seat of Christ, so that each one may be repaid for the things done in the body....
(1 Corinthians 5:10)

ONE OF MY FAVORITE THINGS to do is sit down with a person and get down to the details of life. I want to know their hopes, dreams, fears, and fancies, their favorite movies and songs, the smell of the candle they always burn on their kitchen table...details are so important. I love the connection that comes from knowing someone's life deeply.

Sometimes, though, I think we get *too* close to people, to the point where we start to feel a sort of responsibility or stake in how they live their lives...particularly their walk with Christ. I don't know what it is about Christians, but we tend to be extremely concerned with how *other* people's relationship with the Lord is going...maybe even more than we're concerned with our own.

In my mind—because I'm a very visual person—I see this like Jesus walking down the road with our friend, and we're sort of stepping on the backs of their sandals, trying to overhear everything. We make their walk our walk.

It's good to have Christian community. It's good to have concern for one another, and to correct and reprove when we see others drifting down paths of sin or misconduct. The problem is that many Christians tend to stray into policing how others walk out their entire faith journey. We judge our fellow Jesus-followers on everything from their clothing and music choices to the kind of church or fellowship they attend (if they attend one at all), to the denomination or doctrinal flag they fly. We make it our business to have an opinion on every angle of someone else's walk with the Lord—or maybe just on the parts that are personally really important to us—and we just can't help but get involved whether we're invited or not.

Personal investment aside, when it comes down to it, all the correction, reproof, and advice in the world does not make us responsible for any other Christian's walk. At the Judgement Seat, you will not be held accountable for the behavior of your brother or sister in Christ. Their conduct and choices, and the consequences of these things—for better or worse—are ultimately between them and God. We cannot dictate other people's actions, no matter how badly we may want to. Our focus needs to be much more on our own conduct, our own hearts, and our own calling from the Lord, and how we choose to carry out *our* faith journey, rather than on monitoring everyone else's.

Even with the best intentions in mind, we can very easily lose sight of our own responsibility before the Lord—using our gifts and callings from him to spread the Gospel and minister to the body of Christ—when we become fixated on someone else's life.

Whether in ministerial or relational or other day-to-day situations, in the end, we can only control our own behavior and no one else's. We can give counsel and advice, we can reprimand and take people to Scripture, but the choice is theirs whether to receive or reject reproof or criticism. We can drive ourselves absolutely crazy trying to make it any other way, but that doesn't change the reality that it's up to us as individuals to choose to walk uprightly in every circumstance, because we will be held accountable before our God for our *own* walk and no one else's.

Being accountable for our actions alone is quite the responsibility. So today, I encourage you not to stress about how everyone else on the narrow road is walking. Just concentrate on each step *you* take with the Lord. Lead by example, rather than by being consumed with the behavior of those around you.

This Week's Prayer: God, thank You for this person and the profound walk we share! Thank You for equipping me to walk with You. Help me focus on what You would have me do and where You're leading me, not on what everyone else is doing. Amen.

FOUR STEPS TO FOCUSED PRAYER

Pray without ceasing...
(1 Thessalonians 5:17)

EVER SINCE I WAS A little kid, I've struggled with with being distracted while praying! I'd start to pray, then I'd start to think about whatever I was praying about, and next thing I knew I was just *thinking* about my concerns, not actually *praying*

111

about them. I believe that God still heard the cry of my heart, but my *focus* went from surrendering the matter to taking it back in.

Thankfully, none of us have to be victims of our wandering minds. Scripture tells us that we can lead every thought captive—and that includes those prayers that want to get away from us! Below are four methods that I've found personally helpful when it comes to having a clearer, more focused prayer life:

1. Get Down on Your Knees

Though this practice has been somewhat hijacked by mockers as well as marketing companies looking for an easy way to make a buck on poignant prayer-related posters, the actual action of kneeling in total surrender before the Creator of Heaven and Earth can have a powerful, focusing effect on one's prayer life. It requires us to stop whatever else we're doing, put ourselves in a position of genuflection to God, and stay there until we've brought our supplication before Him.

2. Speak Out Loud

Ever heard someone say, "That sounded better in my head?" Our thoughts tend to wander before we say them, but actually speaking aloud forces us to really *think about our thinking.* Similarly, praying out loud can keep us on a single subject without that thought leading us down a rabbit hole. Praying out loud isn't always an option if you're in a public place or a house full of sleeping family members, but it certainly has its applications in other cases, like in the car while driving to work. The next time you find yourself struggling to stay focused while praying, try doing it out loud!

3. Pray a Recited Prayer

Christians vary widely in their opinions about recited prayers. Some believe them to be no more than a rote repetition of syllables; others consider them the only way to pray with proper reverence. Thankfully, all debates aside, God looks on the heart; for those who struggle to know what to pray for, how to pray, or how to keep their focus while praying, I suggest reading along to the Psalms, Proverbs, or the Lord's Prayer, or even the prayers found in many Prayer Journals and devotionals like this one! This can be a great launching pad toward learning to focus and expand your prayer life. "Praying along" with the words—truly thinking about them, internalizing them, and making them your own as you offer them up to God—can be incredibly helpful in cultivating a deeper focus in your prayer life.

4. Journal Your Prayers

Similar to speaking out loud, writing prayers down can help you stay in the moment so that your mind doesn't wander to other things that derail you. An added bonus to this method is that you can open up these notebooks years later, read the things you prayed about, and see the marvelous and oftentimes unexpected ways they were answered.

It's one thing to read the way God answered prayers in the Bible—it's another entirely to have the inexorable proof right in front of our faces of how He answered *ours*! Journaling of any sort is also a method widely used to combat stress, anxiety, and even panic disorders, all of which can get in the way of a flourishing prayer life. Taking the time to write out a prayer first thing in the morning, right before bed, or even in a few moments of respite during a busy day can be a great focusing technique!

These are just four examples that can help with focusing the mind and taking control of our thoughts during prayer. Different methods work for different people! One of the most wonderful aspects of prayer is that it doesn't *have* to "look a certain way". Prayer is not reserved for a church pew on Sunday; it isn't required to be verbal, written, or simply "thought", and we don't have to be down on our knees to do it. To pray is simply to "ask," and everyone goes about asking in a different way. God looks on the heart and desires genuine relationship with each of us—He hears us whenever we pray, no matter if it's spoken or unspoken. And the wonderful thing about prayer is that the more we do it, the easier it will be, and the more we train our focus, the more readily it comes.

Always remember that God is a Father who meets us where we are at. He is willing to help us along to becoming better prayer warriors and better people all around! All we have to do is ask!

This Week's Prayer: God, thank You for hearing my prayers and my heart, even when I struggle with the words! Help me to become more focused and intentional in my prayers, and please keep me clear-minded and sharp as I practice steps to a more focused prayer life. Amen.

JESUS DIED FOR *YOU*!

**For God so loved the world that he gave his only begotten
Son, so that whoever believes in him will not perish, but have
life in the age to come.
(John 3:16)**

WHAT IS THE MOST GENEROUS thing a friend,
family member, or even a total stranger has ever
done for you? How did it make you feel?

It wasn't until I was an adult that I truly realized what my parents sacrificed so that my brother and I never wanted for anything as children. When I finally understood the depths of their selfless and sacrificial love for us, I had never felt so much gratitude toward them.

I had also never felt more worthy and cherished than I did in that moment of revelation. I saw my value through the eyes of my parents: that they were willing to go without because I mattered to them *so much*.

So did my brother, of course. But one thing that struck me was that, even if it had just been me, as an only child, they would have given up those things for *my* wellbeing.

I remember sitting in a sharing once where the teacher delved into the medical side of the horrific physical agony Jesus endured before and during his time on the cross. If you've never heard this account with all of the gritty medical details included...trust me on this, it's a game-changer.

By the end of that teaching, I was crying just imagining *anyone* enduring so much pain, much less the only person in the history of the world who didn't deserve it.

And for all of that, the part of the teaching that truly stood out the most was when, after all of that graphic description, the teacher looked over his captivated audience and said, "And you know what? Jesus endured that for *you*."

He started to point to some of us as individuals and fill in our names in the blank: "He endured all of that for *you*, Steve. He endured that for *you*, Karen. He endured that for *you*, Rebecca."

I ask you now to reflect on what you felt at that time when someone did something special and meaningful for you.

Was the entire occasion forgettable, or were you inspired by it? If you're like many people, maybe you felt the urge to give back to the other person in some equally-important way as a show of gratitude and appreciation.

That is the kind of response I want to have toward my Savior's sacrifice.

Living for him shouldn't be a chore, but a joyous opportunity to serve the one who gave it *all* for me. Not that he died to accrue favors, but we have been given the ultimate gift through the ultimate sacrifice.

No one will ever do more for us than our brother Jesus did; he suffered unjust torture, he hung from a cross, he gave up his *life* for us. And now he lives again, which means that we have been granted the opportunity, the *privilege*, to serve in his Body with the gifts he imparted to us the moment we accepted that selfless sacrifice as the covering for our sins.

Jesus died for you, [YOUR NAME HERE]. Now it's your turn to live for him!

This Week's Prayer: God, thank You for sending Your Son as the atoning sacrifice for my sins! Jesus, thank you for living out that sacrifice! Please help me to live my life worthy of that incredible, indescribable gift. Amen.

WHAT'S YOUR TREASURE?

For where your treasure is, there will your heart be also.
(Matthew 6:21)

IN MATTHEW 6:21, JESUS ADMONISHED his listeners about the places where they were storing up treasure. I've met many people who carried out the extent of this passage as it pertains to investing their money; they were quick to give and lived a minimalist life. It's easy to assume if we're not clinging to material goods, but giving to the needy and supporting Christian causes, that we're "storing up our treasure" properly.

But I want to challenge us all to consider that there may be another way we're "storing up treasure" unwisely: by neglecting the treasures of **time** and **thoughts**.

My husband compares seconds to cents and always encourages me to "invest" them wisely. I love this analogy because it makes me think of how I only have so many "second-cents" to "spend" in a day. Do I want to fritter them cheaply, or spend them wisely? What's a worthy investment and what isn't?

I'm not saying people need to spend every waking hour of the day reading the Bible. That's just not realistic. Nor do I think every moment of television or "vegging" is poorly invested—sometimes we need to zone out. But as a whole, think about the time you invest in pleasing yourself versus what you invest in the lives of others; the time you invest in spreading Christ's love; the time you spend increasing your knowledge of God's presence, plans, and purposes; the time you spend in the hobbies and giftings that *truly* fulfill your soul. Could you invest more time in these treasures?

Now, our thoughts—the things we dwell on—are precious, because while we actively dwell on them we aren't considering much else. For example, I gave too much mental real estate to unwholesome thoughts as a result (and therefore a perpetuator) of my anxiety.

Our thoughts are treasures in that we decide what we spend our time thinking about and pondering, and as a result we give precedence to those things. It's been proven that the way we think lays the map of our brains. Like a rut, the more we follow one train of thought, the deeper the path becomes, the steeper the sides, and the harder it is to climb out of.

I believe Scripture makes it very clear that our thinking process is important, vital—*treasurable*. God encourages us to dwell on "whatever is true, whatever is noble, whatever is right, whatever is pure, whatever is lovely, whatever is admirable—if anything is excellent or praiseworthy." Why does God care about what we think about? Because where we invest our thoughts, we invest our lives. We are creating maps and paths. We are filling our "mental storeroom" with concepts that our minds will drift toward in idle moments.

How often to you dwell on the darker side of life? Do you give more thought to hope or despair? Do you invest your thinking in true and noble things, or in subjects that make you anxious, angry, and bitter? Could you remap your thinking to focus on things that are more pleasing to God?

We all have ways—some obvious, some subtle—in which we're treasuring up things that are to our detriment, not our benefit. Jesus gave stern warnings after his teaching about treasures: if your eye is unhealthy, your whole body is unhealthy. You cannot serve two masters, like God and money.

If our investment is in unhealthy things, it becomes that much harder to serve God. So take a moment to assess your storeroom. Are you investing your time wisely by God's standards, or neglecting His will for the sake of your own? Are your thoughts darkness or light? Are you carrying useless, or worse, detrimental, inventory?

What are you truly treasuring up?

This Week's Prayer: God, thank You for the precious treasure of thought and reason. Please help me to command and control mine so that my thoughts are good treasure, honoring You! Amen.

A QUARTER-CENTURY IN HINDSIGHT

For everything there is a season...
(Ecclesiastes 3:1)

THE DAY I STARTED TO WRITE THIS PIECE was April 25th, 2018...the day before my twenty-fifth birthday.

Wow. When did that happen? Sometimes I still feel like I'm sixteen. There are times of stress where I look for an adult to handle the situation...but, whoops, I am an adult! I have to make my own doctor appointments, my own dinners, and now I'm raising a family of my own.

Oh, and I can also legally rent a car now. *Watch out, pedestrians.*

In light of this milestone birthday, I began reflecting on the biggest lessons that God taught me in the first quarter-century He had to mold and shape me. And I thought I'd share some of these lessons with all of you:

You Don't Know As Much As You Think You Do

Whether it's doctrinal, scriptural, or relational, God has shown me over and over again through triumphs and failures that there is never a stone that should be left unturned in His kingdom. There have been times I've felt like I've plateaued in my knowledge of the divine—not that I know *everything*, but that I know *enough* for that season of life. And then God has a way of turning everything I *thought* I knew on its head, revealing new mysteries and wonders. He constantly shows me I don't know as much as I think I do, but what's out there to learn is beyond my wildest dreams.

God Works With You As An Individual

As a kid, I loved to learn, but not always in the way my parents insisted we do things! At eight years old, I remember fighting to stay awake as an hour-long teaching CD droned through our stereo speakers. But the older I've gotten, the more I've discovered that I learn the deepest spiritual truths by reading, by being out in nature, by the lessons He brings to mind when I'm writing my own novels, and by listening to music. Endless, endless praise music. After twenty-five years, I finally got to the place where I'm okay with learning at my own pace, in my own fashion—letting God work with me in the way that allows His wisdom to truly reach my heart.

God is Never Done with You

Over the course of that first quarter-century of life, there were many times where I felt like I was at the Spiritual South Pole and God was up there where the Northern Lights shine. I couldn't have felt further away, less worthy, or more like a failure. But consistently and unwaveringly, He waded into the subarctic snows of my self-doubt and yanked me out again. His compassions and mercies are endless and so patient that Scripture says they're *new* each day. No matter how turned-around, lost, and full of doubt I may become—and no matter how wise I may think I am—God is never done with me. He's never done teaching me or rescuing me from my polar pity-parties.

You Need God More, Not Less, As You Age

I've become more and more conscious of antireligious sentiments as I grow older (note to self: stop reading the comments sections on Facebook articles). One of the prevalent remarks I see from nonbelievers is that anyone who believes in God after they hit their teen years is a coward who can't bear to face reality.

My answer to that is...well, yeah. Have you *seen* reality lately? The older I get, the more heavily I find myself relying on the promises and hopes that come from my Father. Not only do I see the world unfolding *exactly* as He said it would—further solidifying my trust in Him—but I also see His love cracking through the hard shell of a world at spiritual and physical war. I see miracles, I see love, I see the promises of God coming true day by day.

With every passing year, the cry of my heart is more to Him than to anything this perverse world has to offer. Time proves nothing so much to me as that the timeless, ageless One is the only hope there is. We need God more as time goes on. Not less.

Time is a Gift

You may think I'm about to get all morbid and go on a spiel about how every second is precious and mustn't be wasted because time goes by *so fast*. While that's one lesson I learned in my twenty-five years, that's not the one I want to share. It's this: time is a gift because if we have willing hearts and flexible vision for our lives, *every day is another chance for God to transform us into His image.*

Day by day, year by year, one quarter-century after the next, we're presented with endless opportunities to live the love of God and Christ, to gain a deeper understanding of our Father, to draw closer with the Body of Christ, to make disciples, work wonders through the gift of holy spirit, worship, pray, fellowship, manifest, and grow. Always grow.

A lot of people see time slipping away as they age. I'm starting to see time expanding. I know exactly how many years I wasted as a teen chasing earthly love, earthly desires, and earthly lessons with earthly outcomes. With the lessons that God has taught me, I'm determined to spend the rest of it chasing *Him* with all my might.

Luckily, Jesus runs beside me, my spiritual and earthly families run beside me, and the finish line is pure promise and hope. That sounds pretty all right to me, and leads to the last lesson:

Never Stop Running

The race keeps going. So must we. Twenty-five was no time to slow down. Neither is thirty, forty, fifty, eighty, or one-hundred-and-nineteen. Keep running after Him in whatever capacity you can. Embrace this time you have to serve Him. Run toward Him. Learn from Him. Work with Him.

Never. Stop. Running.

And here's to the next quarter-century.

This Week's Prayer: God, thank You for the time we have in this life! Thank you that even when it's tough, there is so much we can do for You. Help me make the most of every year, every day, every moment. Amen.

WHAT FOUNDATION ARE YOU BUILDING ON?

He is like a man building a house, who dug deep and laid a foundation on the rock...
(Luke 6:48)

JESUS TOLD A GREAT PARABLE about the wise man who built his house on the rock and the foolish man who built his house on the sand. Both men *wanted* a wonderful place to dwell, and both probably figured they were going about it the right way. One could even speculate that the houses themselves were equally beautiful. But the foolish man's house still crumbled—not because of the house's own integrity, but because he started wrong from the bottom up.

As Christians, a good foundation is essential not just in doctrine, but in conduct, practice, and how we receive the words of our Lord.

There's another kind of "good foundation" I want to talk about today: the daily foundation.

Something that *everyone* seems to struggle with more and more is a sense of dejection, distress, and even hopelessness when confronted with the perils of the world around them. We're constantly inundated with negativity in the religious, political, social, economic, entertainment, and interpersonal spheres. There's almost nowhere we can turn where another punch isn't swinging at our faces.

Sadly, I can't offer a solution for that. What I do know is that the way we start each day—the foundation we build on, if you will—is essential to whether we see these negatives as *overwhelming* or *already overcome*.

God doesn't sugarcoat this subject in His Word: life is going to hit us, and hit hard. But there's great hope in knowing that *greater is he that is in us than he that is in the world*, and that *we will never be left, nor forsaken*, and that *we are more than conquerors*.

Unfortunately, these timeless truths often get buried under the onslaught of negativity. In order to cling to what is good rather than being overwhelmed, one of the best things we can do is **start each day by building a positive foundation**—living a Philippians 4:8 kind of life, for example, which reads:

Philippians 4:8
Finally, brothers and sisters, whatever is true, whatever is noble, whatever is right, whatever is pure, whatever is lovely, whatever is admirable—if anything is excellent or praiseworthy—think about such things.

These things we dwell on, and even *when* we dwell on them, helps to set the day-to-day foundation of our lives. People who start the day negatively have a hard time bouncing back to positivity, whereas the person who dwells on the things that God has deemed true, noble, right, pure, lovely, and admirable has already laid a solid foundation of things to fall back on if their day goes sour.

There's a saying that goes "The life you think is the life you live." I prefer the more historical variation: "A bad tree cannot produce good fruit." In other words, negative produces negativity, positive produces positivity. What kind of tree are you planting and watering? Is your intake bad or good? Do you direct your thoughts to the positive or dwell on the negative?

Everyone has a choice of how to lay the foundation of each day. Choose to begin yours by dwelling on the goodness and glory of God and see how it turns your dark times to light!

This Week's Prayer: God, thank You for providing the tools and supplies to build a great spiritual foundation! Help me make the most of every bit of it, in my thoughts, words, and actions, to build a solid foundation that always endures. Amen.

ONE BODY OF CHRIST

There is one body and one spirit, just as also you were
called in one hope of your calling,
(Ephesians 4:4)

DIVISION IS NOT HARD TO find these days. In
fact, unity is rarer. Ever since the Tower of Babel and
the times of the Patriarchs, humankind has found
increasing ways to divide itself. The Pharisees set

themselves apart from Jesus by their known heritage (casting scorn on Jesus' own conception). The Jews separated themselves from the "dogs" (Gentiles). Some early Christian converts distinguished themselves as followers of "Peter" or "Paul" rather than followers of Jesus.

This practice has continued to modern day. Class, capability, race, political slant and religious choices are just a few of the dividing lines in the sand. Honestly, every unique individual might find themselves encased in a socio-politico-religious dodecagon if all their so-called "dividing lines" were joined together.

The problem with this kind of thinking, of course, is that at its core, it isolates us. Eventually, you could find a way to disagree with every single person you know, and then we all might as well move to deserted islands (separate ones, of course) because we just can't get along.

Sadly, division is as common in Christianity as anywhere else—if not moreso. Where we ought to be modeling the unity of the spirit in the bond of peace, instead our 40,000+ denominations form something more like a divisive rhombicosidodecahedron, where the people on the 20 triangular faces don't interact with the 30 square faces, and the 12 pentagonal faces mutter about the 60 vertices behind their backs, and don't even get us *started* on those 120 edges (they're probably just cults anyway).

There isn't really any hope for Christians all getting on the same doctrinal page before Christ returns, when we'll "know even as we are known," and will see clearly through the glass. Nevertheless, God calls each of us a *child*, His child, and part of *one body*, the Body of Christ.

How often do we take for granted that no matter our denomination, we have spiritual siblings in every single church across the world? Lutheran, Protestant, Catholic, aboveground, underground, safe or secret, persecuted or free, these are *all* our brothers and sisters in Christ. Not just those who fit on our side of one line, but those across other lines of denomination, doctrine, belief, and practice. We are all saved. All sanctified. All following the same Lord, even if we understand him differently based on our theological scope. And yet our focus tends to be on our differences, not our similarities.

Christianity is in a time of crisis. The enemy is ever on the move, and the times grow darker—sometimes by the day. Yet greater is He that is in us (*all of us*!) than he who is in the world. How powerful could Christianity truly be if we focused on what unites us rather than what divides us? What if *we* found a way to look after our fellow Christians as one single tribe?

Because in God's eyes, that's what we are. Neither Jew nor Gentile, male nor female, Protestant nor Catholic, Trinitarian nor Unitarian. We are all Christ's body. He works with each of us, whether we have the "corner" on ultimate truth or not. Part of learning to live the love of Christ in this world must start with loving our brothers and sisters in Christ despite our differences.

In your own life, look at the lines in the sand and find ways to erase them. Reach out to Christians of different denominations. Build bridges. Forge bonds of peace in unity. To the best of *your own* ability, live peaceably with all mankind. And when it comes down to it, above all else, love them like Jesus does.

This Week's Prayer: God, thank You for creating us all equal within Your family! Thank You for creating us for unity in Your name. Help me to tear down any dividing walls in my heart so I can love like You and Your Son and be a force for unity in the Body of Christ. Amen.

THANKFULLNESS: THE KEY TO CONTENTMENT

**For indeed you were called as one body to this *peace*;
and *always* be thankful!
(Colossians 3:15)**

WHILE COUNSELING A FRIEND THROUGH deep discontentment over a lack of feedback on a project she'd put years of effort into, the question arose of what would truly make her happy in this scenario. She could name five people who liked her project; but deep down, she wanted *everyone* to love it. Another friend asked her what would realistically be enough to make her happy.

There was no answer. The silence struck a chord in me: she didn't answer because there is no answer. Because if you can't be content with what you have now, you will not truly be content with anything. It will never be enough

The 2017 movie musical *"The Greatest Showman"* tackles one man's journey from squalor to splendor, and the revelation that no matter how high he climbs, no matter what accolades he receives, he continues to feel empty. He goes from pursuing common favor to chasing the elites of society, then the applause of the nation...but in the end, hollowness and loss force him to come face-to-face with the fact that he had everything he truly needed from the start: a loving family he'd neglected in pursuit of the world's admiration. I love this journey because it shows how, if we aren't thankful for what we have, we will never fill the hole in our hearts.

This is not to say that everyone is in ideal circumstances always, but I would like to suggest that we can find things to be thankful for. Even if it's just the breath in your lungs and the clothes on your back and the opportunity to try again tomorrow, that can be enough. Take the Apostle Paul as an example, who learned to be content in all circumstances through his trust in Jesus. And his circumstances were much of the time far less than ideal!

People often think that if they "just had" *something*, THEN they would be happy and feel fulfilled. If they had x-amount of followers on social media, if they became head pastor of a church, if they found Mr. or Mrs. Right, contentment would be achieved. They think this until they have those things, and the hole's not filled. Suddenly they're left wondering if they had a nicer car, a corner office, kids, pets, maybe *then...*

You get the picture.

Here's the thing: contentment and true joy are not found in achieving success. They're found *in spite of success or failure.* They're found in being thankful for what you have right here and now, not in what you *could* have someday. If your happiness hinges on an outcome, it's not really happiness. It's a pinging pleasure synapse across the lobe of your brain, and once it fizzles out, discontentment will flood back in. You will want the next big thing to make you happy. And the next. And the next. You can actually wire your brain to constantly chase after the Next Big Thing, running toward a horizon that's always moving away from you.

Slow down. Look around. Find contentment in what you have right now and give thanks for that. It's not bad to have goals; it *is* bad to hang your entire outlook on them, though. It's unwise to pin contentment to the notion of a certain outcome rather than learning to live in gratitude with what God has already given you. It's healthy to find contentment and peace in every step of life, because you never know how long you'll be standing there before the next one.

Shift your perspective. Give your eyes a rest from that horizon and bring the closer things into focus. Tally up what you're thankful for *here and now*. It's amazing how much contentment can be found right where we are.

This Week's Prayer: God, thank You for what You have provided for me. Thank You for every blessing in my life. Please help me be content right where I am today, wherever you lead me tomorrow, and to whatever lies beyond that. Amen.

THE VALLEY OF THE SHADOW

**Even though I walk through the valley of the shadow of death,
I will fear no evil, for you are with me.
(Psalm 23:4)**

ONE OF THE MOST COMFORTING verses in the Bible to many Christians is found in Psalm 23: "Even though I walk through the valley of the shadow of death, I will fear no evil, for you are with me."

There is so much hope to be derived from these simple words. Many have taken this verse up as a mantra in times of mortal hardship such as terminal illness, deadly situations, even war. But whether the potential outcome is fatal or not, we all walk through valleys in life:

The valley of illness.

The valley of depression.

The valley of financial burden.

The valley of divorce.

The valley of loss.

Although every valley of the shadow looks different, the God Who walks through them with us is unchanging. The Psalmist happened to be facing an enemy who wanted him dead at the time. But these words ring as true for those who are facing the shadow of broken-heartedness as those who are facing the shadow of their own death.

Your God cares. He is with you. He is beside you. He will not leave or forsake you.

Take a moment to consider your life. What valleys are you in? What shadows do you walk beneath? I encourage you to lift them in prayer today. Lift them to the One who walks beside you through the darkest of the dark. The One whose light pierces the gloom and illuminates the way.

No matter how dim the road, His light shines brighter. He walks with you through your valley, and He will be with you still when you emerge on the other side. His rod and His staff will comfort you. He will guide and guard you forever.

Have trust. Have peace. Fear nothing.

He is with you in *your* valley.

This Week's Prayer: God, thank You for being with me in the valley. Help me feel Your presence like never before. Amen.

PEACE TO THE INCONVENIENCES

*If it is possible, as far as it depends on you, live in peace
with all people.*
(Romans 12:18)

I THINK THE HARDEST THING GOD has ever
asked of me is to live peaceably with all men. I'm
working on improving my reaction to
inconveniences with the help of my Creator, but

there are times when it's so hard not to completely lose my cool and get snippy when things go wrong. Sometimes He has to nudge me back onto the straight and narrow in very specific ways.

Such was the case a few years ago when preparing for a flight to visit a friend. Upon arriving at the airport, we found that our flight was delayed for two hours. As time ticked by, I had what space-rogue Han Solo of *Star Wars* infamy would call "a very bad feeling about this." My tension grew and peace slipped away, compounded when the plane arrived only for the attendants to call those of us with a layover to speak with them.

Uh-oh.

Not five minutes before this happened, my phone buzzed. One of my best friends sent out a Tweet encouraging her followers to do something nice for themselves or others. I was too flustered to think much of it, brushing it off for later. "Yeah, I'll do something nice for myself, like get a cookie on the plane..."

Little did I know, that was a seed.

Over the ensuing half-hour of standing in line, being told we'd miss our connection, and plenty of back-and-forth with the attendants and then my travel companions while we decided what to do, I had a strong sense of the holy spirit moving in me and watering that seed, if you will. Finally, the decision was made: we couldn't make the trip. Distress hit peak heights, the tension headache was starting—

And then I saw her. A harried desk attendant who been a little snappy with us was now leaving her shift. As I watched her walk away, I heard the voice of God: Do something nice for others. *FOR HER.*

I chased her down and thanked her, and her demeanor shifted at once—as did mine. We got to chatting, and it turned out she had to be up and at work again in a little over five hours; since being held back to deal with the dilemma on our flight, she barely had any time to sleep. She and I weren't in such different straits, after all. We agreed to pray for each other, she went home for a well-deserved sleep, and my friends and I caught a cab home.

All weekend, I couldn't stop thinking about that woman, about what had upset her and upset me, and all the inconveniences of life: a missed flight. A traffic jam. A burned dinner. Most of the time, these are mere trifles in the grand scheme of life, but we let them steal our peace so often.

What if we didn't? What if we did our best to make peace with the people creeping into our merge lane at the last possible moment? With the airport attendants who are losing sleep trying to do their job? With our significant other when they make a mistake with our hearts? What if we prayed for them instead of snarling out of earshot? What if we didn't sweat the small stuff, but made peace and amends before we ever lost our tempers?

Jesus had so many chances to lose his cool and make a scene, but he made peace instead. Let's follow his example, imitate his calm, and think of others before ourselves. Let's make peace with our inconveniences and create an environment of peace around us.

Because, after all, "Blessed are the peacemakers, for they will be called children of God." And isn't that what we all aspire to truly be?

This Week's Prayer: God, thank You for bringing calm to times of inconvenience! Thank You for reminding me to represent You well even when things are tense. Help me keep a heavenly perspective when life tries to derail my peace. Amen.

THE IMPERFECT CAN SERVE HIM

But thanks be to God that though you were slaves of sin,
you became obedient from the heart...
(Romans 6:17-18)

IT CAN BE SO HARD sometimes to grapple with
the fact that in our imperfection, our fallen, flawed
state, we are still the representatives of the only man
who ever walked out this messy, complicated life in

perfection. For all my shortcomings, I'm meant to be *his disciple*.

Um—HOW?!

There have been many times in my life where I've felt that I was not worthy to represent Christ until I got my affairs in order. Thus began the long effort to clean up my act so I could serve him.

The problem was that while I was trying to attain some level of inward and outward perfection in order to qualify for service to my Savior, I was neglecting every commission he gave me in the meantime.

Raise your hand if you've ever been there: feeling that you must achieve a certain mark of "goodness" before you will be "good enough" to serve God and Christ.

But here's the thing—and I love this quote: "God doesn't call the qualified. He qualifies the called."

Consider that:

- Moses was slow of speech.
- Paul had a rap sheet that included murder – so did David.
- Thomas doubted.
- Peter denied.
- Jonah fled.
- Esther feared.

And yet God worked with every single one of them.

He helped them walk deeper into the light, away from whatever darkness held them back. They all continued to sin. In some cases, they made life-changing mess-ups even *after* they accepted God's commission.

The point is that we don't *just* serve God once we are cleansed to perfection. In working closely with Him, as 1 Corinthians 3:9 says we must, we become cleaner.

Our fallen state and shortcomings are not something that prevent us from working for our Maker. We should run all the harder toward Him because of them, bringing those rough edges to Him for filing—knowing that in doing His work, we are doing well, and that He wants us as we are.

The longing for perfection—something God does not demand from us in this life, but which we still demand of ourselves—is one of the biggest counteragents to achieving the true will of God.

In the words of renowned photographer Ansel Adams, "To require perfection is to invite paralysis."

So keep moving toward God. Even broken, even hurting, even struggling, He wants to work with us *now*, and He wants us to attain greater levels of understanding, healing, and wholeness as we bask in the light of His perfect love.

It starts with a step. It starts with accepting the call. It starts with surrendering our imperfect selves to God's perfect will, so that the next step in our journey of growth can begin.

This Week's Prayer: God, thank You for calling me to do Your work! Thank You for qualifying me with Your power, not requiring perfection of me. Help me continue moving toward You and operating in Your grace and empowerment. Amen.

5 WAYS TO ENRICH QUIET TIME

"Be still, and know that I am God; I will be exalted among
the nations, I will be exalted in the earth."
(Psalm 46:10)

IT IS A WELL-KNOWN FACT THAT strong
relationships can't be forged without quality time
spent together. To that end, "quiet time"—a space
carved out for prayer, reading, reflection, and

bonding with God—is one of the best methods of spiritual grounding. This time allows Christians to get away from the chaos of day-to-day life, to center and refocus on the things of God. This often involves a dedicated time to pray and read the Bible, speak in tongues, listen for the voice of the Lord, etc.

But for a lot of people, "quiet time" often just becomes a different kind of "chaos time." In the stillness, thoughts take over; we become easily distracted and find that while our bodies may be at rest, our minds are still going a mile a minute in the wrong direction.

If you're one of many who finds "quiet" time to be a lot more chaotic than you'd like, here are a few methods that might be helpful to ground your mind in the "here and now!"

1. Read Something OTHER Than the Bible

This idea is an immediate turnoff for some people. The notion of *quiet time* not involving *Bible time* just doesn't jive for them. But I can speak from experience that sometimes, reading someone else's perspective on a spiritual matter can provide fresh and *refreshing* enlightenment.

There are tons of valuable resources with good, godly messages that can be enriching to one's spiritual walk. Two that I've been deeply impacted by are Lisa Bevere's books and Brene Brown's works. God has gifted many people like these powerful women with abundant wisdom to speak on a plethora of topics. If there's a certain subject that's been on your heart, consider picking up a book by a Christian author that covers that subject from a spiritual perspective. This might open the door for you to learn something new during your quiet time.

2. Go for a Walk

During Christian camps I attended as a teen, one of the things they encouraged during the hour of mandatory quiet time each day was that we walk around the campgrounds. A lot of people found this helpful, as without their headphones in and without their bodies relaxed in a state of rest, they felt revitalized and energetic. Praying became easier, especially as they took in the beauty of God's creation. So if you're feeling bored and sleepy with the same surroundings during your quiet time, consider hitting the sidewalks, a nature path, or your streets, and connecting with God out in His creation.

3. Sip on Something

There may be some biochemical reason for this, maybe not, but in my experience settling in for quiet time has always adopted a sort of special, calming effect when I've done it with a cup of coffee in my hand. Something about that action—as if you're sitting down with a friend at a café—can add a level of intimacy to the experience of meeting with God. If you're in need of a soothing, warm aesthetic to help center your mind as you start your quiet time, consider brewing a fresh cup of coffee, hot chocolate, or tea beforehand.

4. Write Down Your Thoughts

Much like during a silent prayer session, our minds tend to wander during quiet time, which is how we end up with those hectic thoughts I mentioned earlier. One way to eliminate this chaos is to write down what you're thinking. This is a tactic that authors call a "stream of consciousness," where you just jot down whatever comes to mind without trying to make it sound poetic or eloquent. Having a notebook where you write down and organize your thoughts can help you to deal with them and catch when they're straying.

5. Pray a Conversation

I saved the best for last, because this has always been my favorite thing to do during quiet time, something I'd get far away from everyone else to do at those camps I mentioned.

Praying a conversation isn't quite as esoteric as it sounds; literally, it's just conversing out loud with God. While this eliminates the truly "quiet" part of quiet time, it helps keep you focused on what you're saying, how you're saying it, and what the heart is behind it. In my experience, talking to God out loud also helps me to eliminate the sort of stiff, repetitious and overly-religious words that creep into my head when I'm praying silently. If I'm hearing myself talk, I start to sound more like me...I present myself to God as I am, without pretentious catchphrases or wandering thoughts.

There is no "formula" for quiet time. It can look however you need it to. But if you find yourself stuck or searching for a way to enhance, change, or even just start your ritual of quiet time, I hope these five tactics will help you to experience the closeness with God that you're looking for!

This Week's Prayer: God, thank You for the quiet moments we spend together! Help me learn to make the most of these precious times. Amen.

ME & GOD IN A CARDBOARD BOX

So therefore, any of you who does not renounce all that he has is not able to be my disciple.
(Luke 14:33)

WHEN MY HUSBAND FIRST PROPOSED, we were in pretty good shape financially. We had both been blessed to still live with our parents while working full time, so we'd managed to sock away a decent savings. Still, the prospect of living on our own, being solely responsible for bills and rent, was intimidating! We had to have an honest conversation about where to live, what kind of home to rent, etc. After some heavy dialogue about what life would look like if one day we suddenly couldn't make rent, I looked him in the eye and said, "I don't care if we live in a cardboard box under a bridge somewhere, as long as I'm with you."

We've repeated that saying back and forth a lot during our marriage. It's a promise and a reassurance that we're in it for the best and the worst...and it's not an exaggeration for either of us. Of course, living in a cardboard box under a bridge is not what either of us would *prefer*. But it's what we're willing to *endure* if it means sticking together.

There's no doubt I feel that way about my husband. But it suddenly occurred to me to ask myself one day: "Do I feel the same way about God?"

I know I'm supposed to. But am I there yet? Could I be content in a cardboard box under a bridge as long as I had Him? Could *you*?

History is full of examples of people God called into uncomfortable conditions to serve Him. It's easy to *say* we'd do that, that we'd take up our cross and go, while we're sitting in our comfortable armchair watching the sunrise, hot coffee in one hand, Bible in lap, snuggled under a blanket. But if God called us into a situation as uncomfortable as laying our heads on the hard ground every night to serve Him, could we really do it—without grumbling, discontentment, or even resentment toward Him?

This is by no means a call for all of us to sell our things and move under the nearest overpass. But I figure, if I can't give up everything and go where He leads me, then I'm not following Him with my whole heart. I'm not a disciple who could leave the nets and go down the shore in the footsteps of Jesus.

But that's who I *want* to be. I want to be sincere when I say, "Not my will, but Yours be done. Here am I, send me." And if He calls me to a place outside my comfort zone, I want my heart to be willing and ready to follow—to the nearest bridge and beyond.

This Week's Prayer: God, thank You for never forsaking me no matter where I'm at! Thank You for providing for me in every circumstance. Help me to always be content with You whatever comes along in life. Amen.

DIVING INTO THE "DEPEND"

**Trust in the LORD with all your heart, and do not lean on
your own understanding.
(Proverbs 3:5)**

DIFFERENT GENERATIONS SEEM TO HAVE
different qualities they laud and applaud. In times
past it was honesty, integrity, grit, strength;
nowadays, it seems the best thing you could ever be

is *independent.* The ability to care for oneself irrespective of the input of others is considered tantamount to achieving nirvana. According to our modern culture, when you can make it on your own with zero outside influence, that's when you've really made it.

Interestingly enough, humankind was never made to be independent. Certainly there's nothing wrong with becoming capable, skilled individuals, but when we idolize independence as the ultimate achievement, we miss the point that we have Someone bigger than us to rely on...Someone who is greater than any circumstance that could tear down our independence. Someone who is there even when we look away from Him.

In truth, for the Christian there is something that will bring an even greater feeling of freedom than achieving independence, and that is achieving total and complete dependence on God!

That's not to say we must live a life where we refuse to tend to our bills, meet the health and sustenance needs of our family, etc. But the difference between *independence* and *absolute dependence* is that independence relies wholly on the self to be the provider. In other words, when one's strength fails, so does their entire lifestyle, because they have no one and nothing to fall back on. God-dependence, on the other hand, means that we are walking with Him always in wisdom, relying on His strength to guide and lead our steps, and nurturing a relationship of reliance and faith in the good times. That way, when the bad hits, it will be easier to navigate because of the relationship and trust we have already built with Him.

Sometimes, independence can start to look a lot like pride—a total *"I can do it MYSELF because I am all that I need"* kind of mentality. But everyone has their moments of weakness. Everyone has their times when they *can't* do it alone. When those times come, it's better to have trust and reliance on God than to have to navigate our weakness by ourselves.

There's no reason to fear dependence on God. There is nothing wrong with acknowledging our brokenness and learning to rely totally on Him. This level of trust and love between the Heavenly Father and His children is often apparent in third world countries where Christians have next to nothing to their names. They rely on God for everything from providing meals to the miraculous healing of ailments from which they have no defense or cure. And time and again through their testimonies, we see how God honors their reliance by delivering them from sickness, hunger, and death.

It can be challenging to place that much trust and reliance on someone. But God alone knows our deepest needs, our heart's desires, and what will truly profit or harm us in the long run. Independence will eventually leave us isolated and weakened, even devastated when our own strength fails. But if we learn to dive fully into dependence on God, the burden of meeting our every need—as if we ever could!—lifts from our shoulders and into His hands.

This is where our needs and wants are safest. All it takes is fostering trust in Him...and having the courage to dive into the "depend" with God.

This Week's Prayer: God, thank You for being so reliable and faithful! Thank You for providing everything I need. Help me to depend wholeheartedly and unashamedly on You. Amen.

THE RADICAL MESSIAH

And when he came he proclaimed good news of peace to
you who were far away and peace to those who were near...
(Ephesians 2:17)

IN OUR CURRENT VERBIAGE, THE term
"radical" has adopted an unsavory note. It's usually
used to describe someone who's gone off the
religious deep end, or who's pushing some kind of

harmful agenda. But in truth, something is truly "radical" when it relates to or affects the fundamental nature of something, particularly to change it.

So you might say the theory that the earth revolves around the sun was radical to man's belief that the universe revolved around us at the time; or that the idea that the earth itself is round, not flat, was also radical when it was first introduced. There are also people we call "radical"—those who are proponents of a different ideology or belief system than the norm, especially when they're very passionate about it.

You know who was a true radical of his time? Jesus Christ.

It was just recently that I read a Christian book describing Jesus—and his teachings—as *radical*. Not in the surfer/hippy/90's-kid way, but as someone who shook up the fundamental order of his time. Jesus overhauled the way his entire culture related to basically everything from hygiene to interpersonal interactions to God Himself. Jesus' entire ministry *was* radical in every sense of the word.

But the teachings he imparted to his followers were equally as radical as the things he did himself: like turning the other cheek, for example, in a Jewish society that until then operated on the basis of "an eye for an eye"; or loving your enemies and praying for them. These were instructions to be followed by all those who claimed to be his disciples.

Nowadays, that's us. And in these dark times, you can certainly believe that when we follow the radical teachings of our great Teacher, people will take notice.

Think about how the radical love of Jesus can contrast with the culture today. When the social norm is to repay violence with violence or slight for slight, how much attention do you think you can gain for Christ by being loving instead of vengeful? Or when even our denominational boundaries urge us not to reach out to those of different faith-based values, how radical would it be to break down those doctrinal barriers and love one another as children of the Living God?

What about respect? If we respected ourselves and others as beings created in the image of God with worth beyond measure—if we treated others as we want to be treated—how much of our society's arguments over equality would be solved just like that? Just by following one simple command from Christ.

I could go on and on. The teachings of Jesus were not some archaic, Eastern-only concepts which have no application to us today. Every culture of all time is hurting in its own way. Every generation needs a Jesus-revolution—an outpouring of radical love, radical wisdom, and radical change based on the truths he imparted from his Father.

I encourage you to do something radically Christ-like every day, in whatever your sphere of influence may be. See how much the love of Christ can change hearts and lives today, just as it did two thousand years ago.

This Week's Prayer: Jesus, thank you for being a such a life-changer! Thank you for teaching us to follow in your footsteps. Help me to love, inspire, and effect change as radically as you did! Amen.

MAKING USE OF YOUR TALENTS

His lord said to him, 'Well done, good and faithful slave.
You have been faithful over a few things, I will set you over
many things. Enter into the joy of your lord.'
(Matthew 25:21)

I COME FROM WHAT I would call a
"multitalented" family. Everyone in my immediate
circle is blessed with some serious skills, and I'm not

just saying that because I love them. My husband, mom and brother are all gifted artists; my brother is also an extremely talented musician, something he gets from both of our parents; my husband is a jack of all trades and a natural entrepreneur; and my dad, well, he's got the music gift as well as the ability to quickly pick up and be *good* at whatever he puts his mind to, whether it's electronics, cooking, or anything else.

Me, I've always called myself a one-trick pony: I can write. That's it. I can't sing, I can't play an instrument, I can't even draw a mean stick figure. But writing isn't just what I do, it's who I *am*. I believe God has placed stories in my heart to teach His lessons in ways that speak to an audience who would otherwise not be receptive to the messages of Christ. I've been writing since I was very little and there's nothing I'm more passionate about.

But any writer will tell you that a lot of the process goes on behind closed doors, inside your own head.

Growing up, that was a struggle for me. I remember many times I spent gathered with friends who cheered on my brother's piano playing, or when I saw my mom's hand-calligraphed designs in weddings, meetings, and public venues, and I would feel a deep yearning for a talent more tangible than a dozen unfinished drafts growing dust on a computer drive. I didn't want the only thing I was good at to be something I couldn't use to connect with people.

Finally, somewhere in my teen years, I stopped writing other than in sporadic bursts because I felt like nothing I wrote really mattered, anyway. But the nudge stayed. I kept wanting to go back to it, which I realize in hindsight was a God-thing.

Slowly, I eased into the craft again, resigned that I was just going to become a crazy cat lady with my laptop and my coffee cup forever, hoping to write something marketable.

About the time I decided I was okay with that, one of my friends did a teaching on The Parable of the Talents in Matthew 25, where he compared the "talents" (money) that the Master left with the servants to *talents* (giftings) that God has given us. He encouraged us to consider how we're using *our* God-given talents, whether we're making a return on them or burying them.

I thought this teaching was super cool, but I didn't think about applying it to myself.

Funny how that usually happens.

Fast forward almost a year, and once again I was struggling with doubts about writing. My husband and I were reading the Gospels together one morning, as we do, and happened to read Matthew 25. It honestly felt like I was reading it for the first time. I could literally *feel* God opening my eyes to the story of the talents, combining my own doubts with the memory of my friend's teaching and then, last but not least, with the example of my family.

Five talents like my father. Two talents like my husband, mother, and brother. One talent for me.

The Master didn't treat any of those amounts as if they were less important than the other. Whether he gave one servant many or just a single talent, he expected them to make the most of it, to invest rightly, to grow a return.

And right then God struck my heart: I was thinking about burying my one talent, devaluing it and making no use of it.

How could I expect to be entrusted with more if I squandered what was given?

Maybe you've felt the same way at times. Maybe you've seen people around you with giftings that you crave and talents you wish you'd developed. And maybe you *could* develop them with some effort—that's not a bad thing to do!

But I want to encourage you not to bury your talent, your passion, just because it doesn't come with the trappings you may desire.

God entrusts us with our talents for a reason. He expects us to make a return. It may be a difficult, lonely, painful journey, but to invest in your God-given gift and truly make something of it comes with rewards beyond measure. After all, there's no one among us, whether with many talents or just one, who doesn't want to hear at the end: "Well done, good and faithful servant."

This Week's Prayer: God, thank You for giving us all talents to use for Your Kingdom! Thank You for the talent(s) You've given me to steward. Help me to do so in such a way that I am a good, faithful servant. Amen.

GOD OF WONDERS

The heavens declare the glory of God. The expanse shows the works of his hands.
(Psalm 19:1)

IF YOU'RE LIKE ME, THERE have been times when you've looked at the mighty wonders God worked in the time of the Apostles or the Old

Testament and asked yourself why the sun has never stopped or the seas parted in your lifetime.

Have you ever asked yourself if miracles of that majesty, and the intervening hand of God as described in Psalm 18, were a thing of the past?

No judgment if you have. You've got company. I was dwelling on that very thing when the record of Elisha and his servant in 2 Kings 6 struck me in a totally different way than it ever had before.

If you're unfamiliar with this passage, it involves the King of Aram, who was at war with Israel, sending a hoard of soldiers to capture Elisha—effectively to stop him from giving away Aramaean battle tactics by revelation from God to the Israelite king. Elisha and his servant were residing in Dothan and the Arameans surrounded the city while they slept. Imagine the horror in Elisha's servant when he woke to see them surrounded by what the HCSB version describes as "a massive army"! Understandably, he asked Elisha "What are we to do?"

What follows is a passage I've read many times, and I always thought it was one of the greatest examples of a miraculous intervention by God. But for the first time, a certain part stood out to me:

2 Kings 6:16b-17 (emphasis added)
Elisha said, "Don't be afraid, for those who are with us outnumber those who are with them. [17] Then

Elisha prayed, "Lord, please **open his eyes and let him see**." So the Lord opened the servant's eyes. **He looked and saw** that the mountain was covered with horses and chariots of fire all around Elisha.

You know what really strikes me about this passage? Those horses and chariots of fire were already there, already protecting Elisha before the servant's eyes were opened. Possibly they were the only reason the Arameans hadn't already attacked. Yet while they were *present* and doing their duty, the servant was totally unaware until God specifically opened his eyes. He was blind to the spiritual reality before God revealed it to him.

Had Elisha not prayed for revelation for that servant, would he have ever known they were surrounded by chariots and horses who defended them? And would that have made this intervention any less awesome? Like Elisha's servant, are we sometimes unaware of the spiritual forces at work around us? Does our lack of revelation mean that they are not there?

The miraculous, awe-inspiring, mighty hand of God is at work at all times. I imagine that if God opened our eyes to all that He's doing, we would be completely paralyzed with wonder. We look for a sign, but do we need one? Or should our trust be that our God, who is the same yesterday, today, and forever, is working the same wonders both seen and unseen in our lifetime that

He did thousands of years ago in the records that are for our learning and understanding?

I'll leave you to ponder these things with one of my favorite quotes, from Jeffrey R. Holland:

"In the gospel of Jesus Christ you have help from both sides of the veil, and you must never forget that. When disappointment and discouragement strike—and they will—you remember and never forget that if our eyes could be opened we would see horses and chariots of fire as far as the eye can see riding at reckless speed to come to our protection. They will always be there, these armies of heaven, in defense of Abraham's seed."

This Week's Prayer: God, I praise You for Your awesome and mighty power! Thank You for how You use that power to work in, with, and around me. Help me to always be mindful of what a powerful God I serve! Amen.

LIVING THE WARRIOR'S MINDSET

**Put on the whole armor of God so that you will be able to
stand against the schemes of the Devil.
(Ephesians 6:11)**

LISA BEVERE'S "GIRL'S WITH SWORDS" introduced me to the conceptual difference between soldiers and warriors. Bevere makes many great contrasts between these two classes of fighters, but one I found particularly interesting is that while a soldier fights for a specific cause for a duration of time, being a warrior is a way of life. In this analogy, Bevere draws parallels to the *Bushido* code of the Japanese samurai and how their moral and honor code dictated their way of life both on and off the battlefield. The worst thing a samurai could be was a cast-out, masterless *ronin*. Death by one's own hand was preferable to this. Because the samurai lived by one code whether in peace or at war, his conduct was trusted to be above reproach in all scenarios.

Recognizing the difference between the soldier and the warrior mindset forced me to ask myself whether I am living as a *soldier* of God, hired for specific battles as they arise, or as His *warrior*, soul-called to the spiritual fight, speaking out against injustice, standing for those in need, maintaining morality and honor both on and off the battlefield.

The thing about being holy warriors for God is that it is a lifetime commitment. *Wherever* darkness is found, we plunge in and spread light. This is so much more than agreeing to be in the trenches of spiritual warfare for a battle that pertains to our personal interests. It takes training to adopt the endurance and dedication of a warrior such that it impacts every frame of our lives. That sense of honor. That morality. That perseverance. That keenness to see where the conflict is, the courage to move into it at the leading of God and to come out on the other side of it prepared for the next battle. And the next.

When we swear allegiance to God and enter into His family, we have a choice: we can sit on the sidelines and let our belief carry us through; we can get our hackles up for the fights that are of personal significance to us; or we can choose to actively engage everywhere it matters, to champion the cause of Christ, to live and love in a way that is both mighty and gentle—to live as Jesus did. This is what it is to be a holy warrior, not just a soldier in God's army, and to live by God's code both on and off the battlefield. It may be difficult to abide by, but His way is always pure, always perfect, always victorious.

Will you choose to live by that code—the way of the Holy Warrior?

This Week's Prayer: God, thank You for calling me to be a warrior and equipping me for the fight. Help me to live in the mindset of a holy warrior who lives honorably and fights well wherever I am called! Amen.

PRAISING IN THE HARD TIMES

I will call on Yahweh, who is worthy to be praised, and I
will be saved from my enemies.
(Psalm 18:3)

IT'S NOT UNCOMMON TO HEAR THE phrase
"God is good!" in times of plenty. When
circumstances fall together in ways that please and

benefit us, we're often quick to declare the goodness of God because it's right there in front of our faces.

However, the same Christian who praises God's goodness when they drive off the lot in their newly-acquired car might be apt to blame Him when that car crashes. After all, why didn't God stop that from happening? If He was really good, He would have done something about it.

There have been numerous books written on the problem of sin, suffering, and evil, and where God factors into all that. The purpose here isn't to navigate the hows and whys of difficult times, but to encourage all of us that when we face those difficulties, we look to see how God is still working for our good in spite of what we're suffering.

It's rarely easy to turn our eyes from negative experiences in search of the good. Sometimes we need to wallow for a minute and acknowledge that our current circumstances are a struggle! But it better serves us and others if we put the bulk of our effort into thankfulness and finding the goodness of God in such difficult times.

The same God who is good when He opens doors for your dream job or healing in your family is the God who is good when you're down and out, when you feel lonely and hopeless. His strength is made perfect in our weakest times, and He does not abandon us. He is *for* you, and He yearns for your heart, for your wellbeing, for your victory. It will never be harmful to turn *to* Him in these times rather than *away* from Him, to rely on Him and trust His goodness to guide us through the fire.

We are under fire a lot in this world today; sickness, riots, oppression, injustice, death and destruction are commonplace. It can be difficult to find the goodness of God in times like these, yet He is still active, working on behalf of and through His people to the benefit of all.

I encourage you to look for the ways that God is still carrying you, and others, through this tough season. Lean on Him with all your might; you will be stronger for it—and you may even learn of new and amazing ways in which our eternal, unchanging Heavenly Father is indeed so very, very good!

This Week's Prayer: God, thank You for your goodness in both the good and bad times! Help me to never lose sight of that goodness, even when things don't go my way. Please strengthen me to endure always! Amen.

A LESSON IN RESTING

**Come to me, all who labor and are heavy laden, and I will
give you rest.
(Matthew 11:28)**

EVERY WEEK I FIND MYSELF learning new life
lessons just by watching my three sweet kitties, ages
6 to 15. For example, age really is a number—it
doesn't have to stop you from climbing the walls!

Also, if you inhale your food, you're going to have a rough time, every time. And don't ever take a good sunbeam for granted!

Overall, one of the biggest spiritual lessons I've learned from these three cats is the importance of rest.

For those who are not as feline-literate, cats sleep an average of 16 hours a day. God must be a cat-person, giving them that kind of privilege! The thing about a cat is that it doesn't plan its naps based on a schedule; when it's naptime, it's *naptime*. I watch my cats play hard and then sleep hard, faces buried in the nearest pillow or blanket, and I ask myself when was the last time I entered a season of rest when I knew I needed it and not just when it was forced on me by a breakdown after weeks and weeks and *weeks* of crazy on-the-go life?

Our Creator Himself knows the importance of rest. After six days of bringing life to our universe, God rested. Yet somehow I think that I can go a hundred times longer than the God of the Universe before I'll need to stop and catch my breath! And I don't think I'm the only one who constantly feels that there's no *time* for rest. There's just too much to do!

But the pattern of rest is built into our natural world. You can see it in the way animals toil and rest, sleeping when they need to and rising when it's time to chase toys or go outside. An orchid plant blooms and then hibernates until it's rejuvenated. No one has to tell it to rest...it just *does*. Similarly, God instructed the Israelites to let their fields lie fallow every seventh year so that the poor and the animals could pick over them (a season of rest both for the fields and for those who gleaned during this year), and He established the weekly Sabbath so that, just like for Him, there was a mandatory day of rest.

In our busy culture, a day of rest each week isn't guaranteed for the worker—and when it is, we often don't use it to actually *rest*, we use it to catch up on a million things instead. If we aren't active, we feel guilty, like we *should* be doing something. So our times of rest become times of fretting over busyness like a horse at the starting gate, ready to run, run, run.

Like my cats who know when to scamper and when to sit, unapologetic as all cats are, I think it's time we learned to embrace the moment of rest; to breathe in the pause and sink into it; to not hold ourselves in contempt for needing peace. We are made in the image of a perfect and holy God who *also needed a moment of rest*. He designed us to function with pauses in life where we reflect and rejuvenate.

And in case you need to hear it, *you need a season of rest, too*. You need the pause. Listen to your body's signals, to what that quiet inner voice is telling you. Then take the rest, even if it's just your single Sabbath from the stresses of the busy life. Use that time to reconnect with God without all the clamor of responsibilities getting in the way.

Embrace the pause. Embrace *Him*. And rest well, loved ones.

This Week's Prayer: God, thank You for creating me not just to work, but also to rest! Thank You for modeling this way of being. Help me to not feel guilty, but to embrace seasons of rest so I can maximize my effectiveness! Amen.

YOU'RE CALLED HIS

"Fear not, for I have redeemed you; I have called you by
name, you are mine."
(Isaiah 43:1)

LET'S FACE IT: PEOPLE DON'T really like being
labeled. I sure don't want to be a "something," even if
there's nothing inherently wrong in that
"something." I love cats, but I balk at being labeled a

"cat person." And there are far more injurious labels ascribed to people for any number of reasons. Christians are no exception. Besides being called Christians, we're also "Bible-thumpers," "Jesus-freaks," "Holly Rollers" and "Religious nuts," among others. The fear of being labeled a certain way often silences us, since we don't want to be perceived poorly, misunderstood, or mislabeled.

When I was in my teens, this same fear shut me up. Concerned with being labeled a weirdo and a Jesus-freak, I'd never talk about Jesus or offer to pray for someone unless I was in my safe circle of believing friends—and even then, I was reluctant to raise hands in worship, to prophesy or pray in front of people, or to join discussions about the Word for fear I'd do it "wrong".

The older I get, the clearer it becomes that we should be more concerned with whether we're living up to the titles of "disciple", "apostle", "Jesus-follower", and "child of God" than with what *people* are calling us. If God calls us loved, chosen, cherished, *His own*, does it really matter what people call us? No, really—*does it?* Titles can be hurtful, slander and name-calling leave marks, but they are temporal. Our names in the Book of Life...*that's* what's eternal. The name that will be known only to us and Jesus at the end, that's what we should be concerned with being called. Living for God is hard enough without also trying to live up to the understanding and expectations of people. We can't do both. We can't serve two masters.

If we choose to serve God wholeheartedly in the manner that He requires of us, chances are we're going to earn some titles and labels. But so did Christians of every century past. And really, so what? If we are doing the will of God, then we are doing good—even if the world wants to slap a derogatory term on us. It's going to be all right anyway. We have a perfect and wonderful name in the Book of Life and written on the palms of God's hands.

Always remember that whatever they call you, you are still called His. You are inseparably beloved by the Master of the Ages. The rest of it is fleeting pain in a world that is passing away. And *because* you are His, you have so much more to look forward to.

This Week's Prayer: God, thank You for calling me *Yours!* Please help me not to get caught up in what others call me. Help me to keep my focus where it belongs: on You! Amen.

4 WAYS TO HANDLE CONFLICT

"If your brother sins against you, go and tell him his fault,
between you and him alone. If he listens to you, you have
gained your brother.
(Matthew 18:15)

BAD NEWS: CONFLICT IS GOING to happen. It's
been happening even in Christian circles for a long,
long time...think before Christ's ascension! God tells

us that "Your love for one another will prove to the world that you are my disciples." (John 13:35 NLT)

Kind of makes you wonder what our contention among ourselves proves to the world.

Much as we strive to live the love of Christ, it's impractical to think we won't have disagreements in his Body. So the matter becomes not that we have disagreements, but rather that the way we *handle* them, will stand out as a stark witness of whose we are. Are we God's, or are we our own—fighting for the proud and fleshly desire to be right and justified, to have the last word, to prove we are above reproach?

In pondering that, here are four important things we can do when faced with conflict that will help us to be good witnesses, and not poor examples, of the One we serve:

1. Don't React in Anger

Slow down. Take deep breaths. If possible, put some time and distance (not too much, but enough to cool down) between you and the offense that started the conflict, and try to look at it in a practical way. Don't take the contention straight to other people for their insight—that often leads to gossip. Take it up with God first and ask Him what HE would have you do about the situation. Consult His Word as well for the wisdom He's already laid out.

2. Remember that Jesus is FOR this person, not against them

Remembering how Jesus views the other person doesn't automatically mean they're right. But it does mean that Jesus loves them fiercely, even if they're wrong; which also means that Jesus is fighting for their wholeness and both their temporal and eternal joy, just as he's fighting for yours. Remember too that this person is not your enemy, and that your fight is not against them. It's amazing the shift that can happen when we look at the person we're in conflict with through Jesus's eyes, and love them with his love. Human love has its limits. The love of Christ does not— not even in the face of conflict.

3. If this is a brother/sister in Christ, they must be treated accordingly.

There is no way around this. Even if they swung the first punch, that is something they must answer to God for. No matter how much your fellow Christians antagonize, aggravate, or hurt you, they are still family in Christ. That means we're given a strict rule to love them. Easier said than done at times, but God gives no permission for us to retaliate in sin just because we're hurt and/or righteously angry. We're to conduct ourselves in specific ways when in contention with a brother in Christ (Matt. 18; Rom 12:17) and when working to handle conflict, we have to check our conduct frequently, if not constantly, against the godly parameters laid out in Scripture.

4. Seek Resolution, Not Revenge

Our carnal nature is a real get-backer. It wants to repay eye-for-eye, like our pre-Gospel ancestors living under the Law. But Jesus changed the rules when he told us to turn the other cheek. That doesn't mean we need to let conflict eat at us, or be passive and just take offense as if it was all our fault it happened. Instead, in this instance, seek a peaceful resolution rather than to outdo the other person in harsh words, actions, or slander (Rom. 12:18). If someone goes to other people talking poorly about you, don't go to those same people and stir the pot. Make your statements clearly and concisely, and as much as it's in your power, try to reconcile. Taking the high ground of a peaceful solution in conflict rather than a defensive one often says more about our character than if we rush around putting out small fires with individual people.

Above all, having the love of Christ in the face of conflict means that we are seeking the other person's wellbeing. It means that we are not out to smear their name and prove they're wrong, but to bring about redemption—interpersonally, and for the individual. Because the love of Christ is other-focused, it seeks to heal and restore, not to tear down and prove a point.

We can't necessarily solve every conflict through our love alone—there's another party involved, after all, with the free will to choose whether *they* will walk in the love of Christ or not. But we can be confident that we did our best to bring about a godly resolution and fought for the other person as much as possible when we imitate our Savior in times of conflict, just as in times of peace.

This Week's Prayer: God, thank You for being present in times of conflict! Help me always seek to resolve differences in ways that glorify You and bring a good witness for Your family Amen.

BREAKING DOWN WALLS

For he is our peace, who made both groups into one and
has broken down the dividing wall, the partition between us.
(Ephesians 2:14)

ONE SUMMER, I VISITED CHICAGO with a group
of friends. It was my first time visiting a truly *big* city in
many years, and let me tell you, it was tiring after three

days! But I went into it with a prayer that God would use the experience to teach me something new.

What He showed me was that as much as I want to see people the way Jesus does...I really don't.

Throughout our stay, we crossed paths over and over with people I found myself making assumptions about. The way they would look at me or my friends, whisper among a group, or even their very posture as we passed by sent me jumping to conclusions about what they were thinking, how they were judging us, and even wondering if they meant us harm. (None of this, by the way, felt like revelation from God. Just my humanity getting in the way of seeing people how Christ sees them.)

Throughout that stay, I found myself thinking about how the penchant for this kind of reactive judgement is not limited to big-city visits. It happens all the time, often in subtler, sneakier ways, so that we're not necessarily aware we're doing it.

But consider how long it might take you to assign motives to someone's actions when you first hear about something they said or did. Is your first instinct reactive, or considerate? Are you swiftly convinced you know what the other person is thinking or exactly what they meant, or do you allow for the possibility of a misunderstanding and pursue the truth with them?

I can tell you for sure that in my own head, I tend toward the former. When I'm counseling my friends, I tend toward the latter. But I'd rather be slow to judgement and quick to assume the better of someone to avoid hardening my heart and damaging a relationship.

All in all, this experience caused a shift in my prayer: I've asked God to help me slow down, to not assume I know what someone is thinking or feeling or what they'll do or say to me. This volatile tendency puts up barriers between people, because in our heads we already have the individual all figured out.

But how can you effectively minister to or be in relationship with someone if you have this determination of who and what they are before you've even scratched the surface with them?

We may not even be aware of all the ways in which our understanding is blinded, all the subtleties of how we size up and separate those around us and create barriers that stanch our effective witnessing for Christ.

But God can reveal those blind spots to us—and what's more, He is perhaps the only One who can truly help us break down those walls so that they no longer hinder us from spreading His Word, His love, and the glorious good news about His Son to a world that so desperately needs it.

Whatever other conclusions we draw in the spur of the moment about others, that is certainly the one truth universal to all people: they desperately need Jesus.

Let's start by seeing that need, and meeting it with our words, our actions, and the love of Christ.

This Week's Prayer: God, thank You for Your abundant love! Please help me see others through Your eyes. Help me see hurts that need healing and needs that can be met, so I can help lead them nearer to You! Amen.

THE BREWER, THE SERVER AND THE SERVED

Jesus answered and said to her, "If you knew the gift of God, and who is the one who is saying to you, 'Give me to drink,' you would have been the one to ask him, and he would have given you living water."

(John 4:10)

THERE ONCE WAS A BREWER who inherited from his father the recipe for the most perfect drink ever consumed by man. Everyone who drank it tasted different notes—saffron and nutmeg, clove and cardamom. For some, these tastes went down bitterly; yet the aftertaste was gloriously sweet, and no one who left after tasting the drink was dissatisfied or thirsty in the least.

News of this perfect brew spread, and the brewer invited anyone with an appetite for a drink to come have a taste. The only stipulation was that you had to drink at *his* establishment. There was nowhere else that this perfect drink could be found.

As word got around, people came from far and wide to sample the brew. And as the establishment flourished and grew, the brewer had to hire servers to help him distribute the high demand for the drink. All were welcome to apply who were interested in satisfying the thirsty populace.

Business was booming. People were satisfied and sent away happy.

And then, one day, the brewer walked out to find one of his long-time servers preparing a pitcher of the drink—and watering it down. He stopped the man and asked him what he was doing, and the server answered with a smile, "Well, the drink is great, there's no denying that. But a few people were complaining that the spices were too strong. I decided to water it down to be more palatable. That will just increase your revenue, since people don't want to come for a drink that's harsh to the palate."

The brewer smiled sadly and shook his head. "I know that the brew burns going down. That's the point. What's beneficial for us is not always easy. But I gave you something that was perfect and pure and true. What you're offering them isn't the real brew...it's an imitation. True, it will never cause them discomfort...but it will also never really satisfy them. Is it worth giving them an imitation of the greatness simply because it's more comfortable for them?"

The brewer asked a good question, didn't he? Why would we ever water down what is pure and true, even if it hurts—like a Gospel message that calls for repentance and change—just to give people something painless...something that will not fulfill their hearts or set them free?

This Week's Prayer: God, thank You for giving us Your true and perfect Word! Please help me to never water it down for mine or others' comfort. Help me to spread Truth in all its perfection without fear or shame! Amen.

About
R.S. Dugan

R. S. Dugan joined the Spirit & Truth team as a volunteer in 2008 and has since become a staff member assisting with administration, heading up the Writer's Network, and contributing to the content pool with written works of her own, which is her greatest passion both on and off the job.

An Indiana native, wife, and mother, she is excited to share that passion with future generations and with her own, particularly through the written word. In her free time, Renee loves writing novels, spending time with her family and friends, and visiting every small-town coffee shop she can find.

About
Spirit & Truth

SPIRIT & TRUTH is a worldwide, multimedia, multigenerational learning platform helping people become like Christ together through videos, podcasts, articles, blogs, social media networking, a Bible translation and commentary project, a virtual learning center, online and local fellowships, regional and national events, and more. This effort is spearheaded by a team of varying ages from different walks of life and backgrounds, unified around the goal of helping people experience transformative relationships with God, Jesus Christ, themselves, their families, and the Body of Christ.

OUR MISSION

We provide sound, biblically-based teaching, transformative learning experiences and support to self-organizing communities to give people throughout the world the opportunity to be saved and come into a knowledge of the truth.

We inspire people to enter into transforming relationships with Jesus Christ, their Father God, themselves and their Families, so that they are able to fulfill their functions and edify the body of Christ in love to the praise of God's glory. We are committed to leading the way in demonstrating how to keep the unity of the spirit in the bond of peace among all in the body of Christ.

www.spiritandtruthonline.org